Quilted
Projects

FROM SCRAPS AND STASH

QUARRY

Quilted Projects

FROM SCRAPS AND STASH

Crazy Quilting, Collage, and Embellishments

GLOUCESTER MASSACHUSETTS

QUARRY BOOKS

BETTY AUTH & CANDIE FRANKEL

First published in the United States of America by

Quarry Books, an imprint of

Rockport Publishers, Inc.

33 Commercial Street

Gloucester, Massachusetts 01930-5089

Telephone: (978) 282-9590

Fax: (978) 283-2742

www.rockpub.com

Library of Congress Cataloging-in-Publication Data
Auth, Betty.
    Quilted projects from scraps and stash : crazy quilting, collage, and embellishments / Betty Auth and Candie Franke.
        p.   cm.
    ISBN 1-56496-983-5 (pbk)
    1. Quilting. 2. Quilted goods. 3. Fancy work. 4. Crazy quilts. I. Frankel, Candie. II. Title.
TT835.A9444 2004
746.46—dc22   2003019317
                                                                    CIP

ISBN 1-56496-983-5

10 9 8 7 6 5 4 3 2 1

Book and cover design: kelly**design**
Layout and production: Susan Raymond
Photography: Brian Piper Photography
Cover photo: Bobbie Bush Photography, bobbie@bobbiebush.com
Illustrations: Judy Love

Printed in Singapore

In memory of
Betty Auth
(1934–2002)

I never knew Betty Auth, but from what I hear, the loss was mine. Betty died unexpectedly in December 2002, with her work on this book well underway but not yet complete. In a certain way, this book is a culmination of Betty's lifelong interest in collecting and creating with scraps and stash. People have told me that Betty loved doing creative work and that she had many more projects left in her. I have endeavored to bring this final project of Betty's to a conclusion she would find satisfying. The contributing artists join me in wishing her farewell.

—CANDIE FRANKEL

Contents

Introduction

Quilters and needle artists share a common passion. We love to collect fabrics. Au courant prints, vintage silks, 1940s barkcloth—beautiful fabrics like these cross our paths all the time, and we can't help but gravitate to them. We are notorious for amassing huge stashes of fabrics and notions that we know we will use, eventually. When a friend's diligent rummaging turns up an unusual print, we're apt to blurt out "Oh, I've got some of that" before realizing the full implications of our confession.

The instinct for stash building comes naturally to those who enjoy crazy quilting and fabric collage. Some might argue you either have the gene for it or you don't. Basically, it's about seeing the potential. You're browsing at a rummage sale and come upon a badly stained, torn tablecloth. But wait a minute. What about those beautiful hand-embroidered flowers in the corners? Vintage fragments like these simply must be rescued. A well-rounded stash includes scraps of embroidery, loose quilt blocks, doilies, ribbons, trims, buttons, and other odds and ends of the sewing trade. We stockpile these treasures, knowing that one day it will be especially satisfying to integrate someone else's past work—even her unfinished work—into our new pieces.

This book introduces the work of quilt and fiber artists who fight the battle of the fabric bulge head-on. The projects may be small, but the ideas run big. The idea is never to use up (we'd only go shopping again) but to make creative withdrawals, to experiment with bits and pieces of fabrics and trim, adjusting and manipulating them to our hearts' content. Just as a musician warms up with scales and études, and a painter makes dozens of preliminary sketches, a quilter needs small sewing projects to continually exercise her eye-hand-stash coordination.

These small projects are truly risk-free. They let you play with various colors, shapes, and textures unhampered by the commitment that a big quilt project requires. Should you visualize a larger piece or multiples, a single small project can serve as a tryout version. You can incorporate your own small quilting samples and practice pieces into many of these projects. The small size often translates into portability, particularly for embellishment work that is done by hand.

No matter where the treasures in your stash originated, this book offers lots of ideas and instructions for transforming them into beautiful, useful items for yourself or for others. You will find machine and hand quilting, photo transfer, embroidery, and a generous sampling of crazy quilting and collage—a wealth of ideas waiting for your creative hand.

Basics

An overview of materials and techniques
to help you rediscover a long-lost
skill or learn something new

What You'll Need

The heavy equipment in your quilting studio will, of course, be a **sewing machine**, a **steam iron**, and an **ironing board**. Treat your sewing machine to a professional tune-up once a year, and follow the manufacturer's recommendations for routine maintenance. For today's quilters, a rotary cutting set, consisting of a rotary cutter, a thick acrylic cutting ruler, and a self-healing cutting mat, is mandatory for big quilting projects. You will find rotary cutting tools handy, but not essential, for the projects in this book. You will need top-quality **sewing shears**; be sure to reserve them for fabric cutting only.

For handwork, including plain sewing, quilting, embroidery, and beading, you'll need **needles**, a **thimble**, **small scissors**, **straight pins**, and a **seam ripper**. Embroidery and quilting **hoops** are used to hold the fabric taut. Use screw-tightened hoops for a firm grip; if slipping persists, wind strips of organza or batiste fabric around the hoop.

Your needle collection will evolve as you try different techniques and threads. Keep a selection of sharps (for plain sewing) and embroidery, quilting, and beading needles in different sizes. Choose the needle type according to the type of work you are doing. Choose the needle size according to the thread the needle will carry. For smoother sewing and minimal stress on the thread, use the finest needle that can be comfortably threaded. A size 3 embroidery needle, for example, is appropriate for six strands of cotton floss. If you are using three strands, the smaller size 8 needle is better.

NEEDLE TYPE	DESCRIPTION	SIZES	USE THIS THREAD
sharps	average length, small eye	1–10	sewing, silk
embroidery	sharp point, long eye	1–10	cotton floss, pearl cotton, metallic thread, rayon floss, narrow silk ribbon
quilting	short length, tiny eye	5–10	quilting, sewing, silk
beading	long, smooth shaft; long, narrow eye		Nymo, silamide, silk, polyester

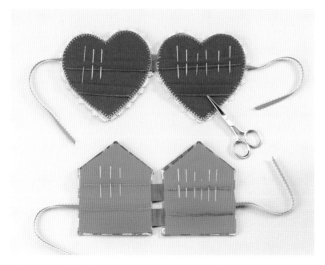

Use a needlebook to store your needle collection.
See the project on page 20.

There are many beautiful **threads** to use for handwork: cotton and rayon flosses, pearl cotton, silk sewing thread, silk buttonhole twist. Fine silk ribbon is in a class by itself. Vintage threads can be used, as long as they are strong and viable. Test the thread; if it breaks frequently, tangles, or gives you other problems, resign yourself to finding something else.

Other items to keep on hand include basic **office supplies** (paper, pencils, tape, paper-cutting scissors), **measuring and marking tools** (tape measure, steel ruler, fabric marking pens, permanent pens), liquid and fusible **adhesives**, and a **craft knife**.

Read the project instructions to find out which materials and tools you will be needing. For leads on where to buy specific items used in the project, see the Product Resource Guide on page 110.

MAKING AND USING TEMPLATES

Some projects require **templates**. A template is a cardboard or plastic cutout of a project pattern. By tracing around the cutout, you can mark the pattern shape on fabric. Templates can be used over and over, making it easy to make multiples of a favorite project.

To make a template, lay **template plastic** over the pattern and trace the outline with a pencil. Then use scissors to cut out the shape on the marked outline. Another way is to photocopy the pattern, glue the photocopy to thin cardboard, and cut out the shape. If a pattern needs to be enlarged, use a photocopier. Set the copier's enlarger feature to the desired percentage.

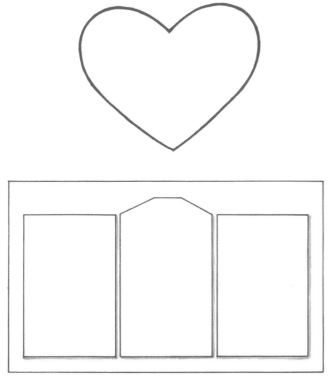

Above: Heart and triptych template shapes.
Right: Sketching a project idea.

Simple template shapes that are based on rectangles are easy to draft yourself. In addition to a pencil and a ruler, you'll need a drafting triangle or graph paper. Follow the project instructions to draft the basic shape and any additional lines.

MARKING FABRIC

There are several ways to mark fabric for sewing.

- Insert **straight pins**. Pins make quick and handy markers. The downside? If they come out, you've lost your mark. Watch for finger pricks, too.

- **Hand-baste** in a contrasting thread color. This method takes time, but it's accurate. Pull out the basting threads at the completion of the project.

- Use a **disappearing marker**. Air- and water-soluble fabric markers are easy to use, but they are not foolproof. Always test them on a sample of your project fabric to make sure the marks truly will come out.

- Use **dressmaker's carbon** and a **tracing wheel**. If you can handle a rotary cutter, rolling a tracing wheel will be easy. Tiny points on the wheel leave behind a dotted chalk line that brushes off of most fabrics.

PHOTO TRANSFER METHODS

Photo transfer onto fabric has given many quilt and fiber artists a tantalizing new medium to explore. At the touch of a button, color photocopiers, scanners, and printers can enlarge, reduce, crop, or reverse any image that is fed to them. Add digital cameras to the mix and the possibilities for personal expression multiply. Several easy photo transfer methods are used to make the projects in this book. The methods are interchangeable as far as the projects are concerned. Which method you choose will depend on the equipment and materials available to you.

The **heat transfer method** requires special heat transfer paper, a photocopier or computer printer, and an iron. Copy or print the image in reverse onto the heat transfer paper. Position the transfer paper facedown on the project fabric, and iron on the wrong side in a circular motion. The transfer will adhere within a minute or two. For a matte finish, peel off the paper backing while it is still warm. For a shiny finish, wait until it is cool.

The **inkjet-printing method** requires special inkjet-printable fabric and an inkjet computer printer or inkjet copier. The special fabric feeds through the computer printer or copier just like a sheet of paper. Rinsing and air-drying the printed fabric makes it colorfast.

The **liquid transfer medium method** takes longer than the other methods but is less expensive. Copy or print the image in reverse on plain paper. Smooth the liquid transfer medium over the copy with an old credit card. Turn the wet copy facedown onto the project fabric, pressing or rolling lightly to make sure the transfer medium makes smooth, uniform contact. Let set for 24 to 48 hours, or until dry. To expose the transferred image, saturate the paper backing with a damp sponge and peel it off.

For transfers with a soft, timeworn appearance, try **Lesley Riley's method**. Long before special transfer papers or mediums became available, Lesley was experimenting on her own using an inkjet printer and matte medium. Start by printing the image in reverse on an inkjet transparency. Fuse an iron-on fabric stabilizer to the wrong side of white fabric, but do not remove the paper backing. Apply matte medium to the right side of the fabric and smooth it out with your finger. Feel for very wet or very dry areas as you go, to ensure the surface is uniformly covered. Lay the transparency ink side down onto the medium. If the medium is just the right consistency, the transparency will stick. If it is too wet, the transparency may slide and smear and you will have to start over. Immediately rub the back of the transparency with your finger or a burnishing tool, pressing firmly. Once the entire surface has made contact, you can apply more pressure in some areas for a well-defined transfer or less pressure for a softer effect. To remove the transparency, peel it up by one corner. Let dry, and then seal with another light coat of matte medium. This method is fun to use if you like variation, unpredictable results, and happy accidents.

CRAZY-PATCH

To create the helter-skelter look of crazy-patch, you'll need to follow a game plan. Start with a muslin foundation and scraps of fabric. Silks, taffetas, and velvets are especially suited to this technique. The muslin should be prewashed, ironed, and cut at least 1" (3 cm) larger all around than the desired finished size.

Cut a scrap of fabric into a five-sided shape, making the edges and angles as diverse as possible. Pin the shape right side up to the middle of the muslin foundation. Place a second fabric scrap facedown on the first fabric and align it along one edge. Machine-stitch ¼" (0.5 cm) from the edge through all three layers.

Flip the second patch right side up, over the seam allowance, and finger-press. Trim the second patch to create a new shape. Continue stitching new patches to the work, one by one, striving for contrast in color, value, or texture. Build out from the center, trimming each patch with the future seam lines in mind. For more complexity, or to gain more seam lines for embellishment, sew two smaller patches together and add them as a unit. If you find you can't maneuver out of an awkward spot, hand-sew a patch or two to finesse the situation. Continue until the entire muslin foundation is covered.

Use embroidery and beading to embellish the seams of crazy-patch. Buttons, ornamental pins, lace trims, and similar embellishments can also be added to the seams and within the patches.

EMBROIDERY

Embroidery is a form of decorative hand sewing. It requires a sharp-pointed needle with a long eye. The sharp point is necessary to pierce the fabric. The long eye accommodates decorative embroidery threads, which are typically more bulky than plain sewing thread. You can embroider with cotton or rayon floss, pearl cotton, silk thread, and silk ribbon, all of which come in varying sizes. Silk ribbon embroidery in particular brings a unique, lustrous dimension to your needlework projects.

There are many embroidery stitches to choose from, and most are very easy to learn. Once you've done a stitch a number of times, your fingers tend to "memorize" it. A sample or picture of the stitch is enough to jog the memory. If you've never embroidered before, ask at your local public library or needlework shop for an illustrated instruction booklet.

BEADING

Beading on fabric is typically done with small, lightweight beads such as seed beads, bugle beads, and rocailles. Beads can be matte or shiny, opaque or transparent. Rocailles are square-holed, silver-lined beads that are especially brilliant. Of course, when you're adding beads to a piece collage-style, just about any bead can be a candidate.

To sew beads to fabric, you'll need a beading needle and beading thread. Beading needles are long, thin, and pliable. The eye is very tiny and the needle shaft does not bulge out around the eye as it does on an embroidery needle. This ultra-slim profile

EMBELLISHMENT SAMPLER

allows the needle to pass through the tiny bead holes unimpeded. Embroidery silk, Nymo beading thread, silamide, or a strong polyester thread are all good thread choices. Try to match the thread content and color to your fabric.

Use the tip of the needle to pick up the beads. Beads can be sewn onto the fabric one by one using a backstitch, or several beads can be strung together in a short run and couched down. You can mark a design for beading, follow a design in the fabric, or work freestyle. You can also combine beading and embroidery.

Vintage Fragments

THE RESOURCEFUL NEEDLE ARTIST
LOVES TO RECYCLE YESTERDAY'S REMNANTS
INTO NEW TREASURES.

Embroidered Needlebooks

Andrea Stern

ARTIST

ABOUT THE VINTAGE FRAGMENTS

At flea markets, antique malls, and similarly irresistible places, you may happen upon a basket of embroidered linens. Sort through them with a judicious eye. Instead of looking for perfect items at lofty prices, hunt down samples that are stained, tattered, and torn. Designer Andrea Stern liberated snippets of precisely such "hopeless" pieces to create her contemporary needlebooks. Pretty and also practical, these little holders keep your needle collection safe and handy.

Fragments of embroidery are perfect for decorating needlebooks. Consider them the perfect advertisement for all the creative work you and your needles are waiting to perform. Don't be snobbish about including machine-made embroideries. They can add wonderfully complex textures, colors, and patterns to your creations. These three needlebook projects—a padded heart and two variations—contain design elements that can be combined in a variety of ways.

VINTAGE FRAGMENTS

- red-on-red machine-embroidered fabric
- machine-made flower appliqué
- hand-embroidered bird with pinked edges

MATERIALS FOR PADDED HEART

- 1 fat quarter hand-dyed red fabric
- 8 ½" x 11" (22 cm x 28 cm) deep red felt
- scrap of linen fabric
- 1 yard (0.9 m) narrow white lace or eyelet trim
- ½ yard (0.45 m) narrow red picot-edge ribbon (for ties)
- 5" x ⅞"-wide (13 cm x 2 cm) red grosgrain ribbon (for hinge)
- variegated red embroidery floss
- gold bugle beads
- beading thread
- sewing thread
- photo or image of face (for photo transfer)
- low-loft polyester batting
- fabric glue

TOOLS

- sewing machine
- steam iron
- photo transfer supplies (see page 14)
- sewing shears
- pinking shears
- small, sharp scissors
- needles: sharps, embroidery (#2 crewel), beading
- straight pins
- seam ripper
- turning tool
- presscloth
- fabric marking pen
- template-making supplies (see page 12)

INSTRUCTIONS

Making the Padded Covers

1. Use the heart patterns on page 23 to make 1 Large Heart template and 1 Small Heart template.

2. Cut 2 pieces of hand-dyed red fabric and 2 pieces of batting, all 7" × 7" (18 cm × 18 cm) square. Place a red fabric square facedown on your work surface. Set the Large Heart template on top. Use a fabric marking pen to trace around the heart outline. Use a seam ripper to cut a 2" (5 cm) slit well within the heart outline.

3· Place both red squares right sides together, with the slitted heart on top. Layer them on top of the batting squares. Pin through all layers. Machine-stitch on the heart outline all around. Stitch again all around to reinforce the seam.

4· Turn the sandwich over. Using small, sharp scissors, trim the excess batting as close to the stitching line as possible. Trim the excess fabric ¼" (0.5 cm) from the stitching line. Clip the curves. Carefully turn the heart right side out through the slit opening. Use a turning tool to poke out the point and smooth the curved edges. Use a steam iron and presscloth to press the heart flat.

Stitching the layers

LARGE HEART

SMALL HEART

5. With the slit on the underside, topstitch ⅛" (0.3 cm) from the edge of the heart all around. Thread a #2 crewel needle with 6 strands of floss. Embroider cross-stitches in a random pattern through all the layers, for a quilted effect. (Felt needle holders will conceal the underside of the work.) Sew white lace trim around the edge, by hand or machine, to conceal the topstitching. Repeat steps 1–5 to make a second padded heart to match.

Quilting and Trimming

Embellishing the Front Cover

1. Place the machine-embroidered vintage fabric facedown on your work surface. Set the Small Heart template on top, and trace the heart outline. Cut out the heart shape with pinking shears.

2. Use a photo transfer method (see page 14) to copy your face photo onto linen fabric. Use pinking shears to trim the image to 1¼" × 1¼" (3.5 cm × 3.5 cm) square, cropping in on the face.

3. Place one of the padded hearts right side up. Center the small heart right side up on top. Stitch in place by hand or machine. Center the face on the small heart and stitch it in place. Use a beading needle and thread to hand-sew gold bugle beads around the small heart, about ¼" (0.5 cm) apart, so that they radiate outward.

Assembly

1. Lay both hearts side by side, about ½" (1 cm) apart, with the slits facing up. For the hinge, run the grosgrain ribbon across both hearts as shown. For the ties, place an 8" (20 cm) length of narrow ribbon at the outside edge of each heart. Use fabric glue to attach all the ribbons. Let dry.

Gluing the Hinge and Ties

2. For the needle holders, cut 2 hearts (use the Large Heart template) and four 1" × 5½" (3 cm × 14 cm) strips from red felt. Lay the felt hearts flat. Fold the strips in half lengthwise. Place 2 strips horizontally on each heart, about 1" (3 cm) apart and with the folded edges at the top. Pin in place. Zigzag each strip along the lower cut edges through all the layers. Trim off the excess at each end even with the edge of the heart. The strips will hold the needles.

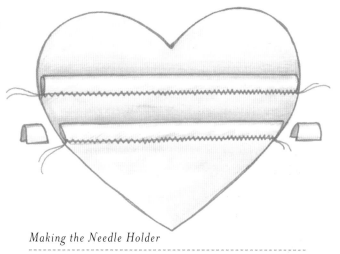

Making the Needle Holder

3. Align a felt heart on the wrong side of each padded heart, concealing the slit. Pin in place. Thread an embroidery needle with 3 strands of floss.Embroider blanket stitch around the heart edges to join the pieces together.

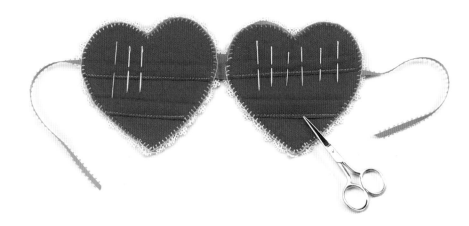

Heart Variation

In this variation, the front and back covers are stiff rather than padded. You'll need two 8" × 8" (20 cm × 20 cm) pieced quilt blocks, a scrap of linen fabric, and a vintage fragment appliqué.

Trace 2 hearts (use the Large Heart template) onto matte board or cardboard. Cut out the hearts using a craft knife. Use fabric glue to affix a heart cutout to the wrong side of each quilt block. Trim the block ¾" (2 cm) beyond the heart outline all around. Fold the excess onto the back of the cutout and glue down. Glue lace trim around the edge. Mark a smaller heart (use the Small Heart template) on the linen fabric and cut it out with pinking shears. Glue the linen heart and vintage fragment appliqué to the front cover. Follow the Assembly instructions on pages 24–25 to complete the project, except glue the needle holders in place instead of securing them with blanket stitch.

Front Cover

Back Cover

House Variation

For this variation, you'll need a House template (use the pattern below) and two contrasting fabrics—one for the house and one for the roof.

Use the House template to trace 2 houses onto matte board or cardboard. Cut out the houses using a craft knife and metal straightedge. Stitch two contrasting fabrics right sides together, making a straight seam. Press the seam allowance open. Use fabric glue to affix the house cutouts to the wrong side of the fabric, letting the seam line represent the eaves. Trim the fabric ¾" (2 cm) beyond the house outline all around. Fold the excess onto the back of the cutout and glue down. On the front, glue narrow trims over the seam. Glue on the vintage fragment. Follow the Assembly instructions on pages 24–25 to complete the project. Use two grosgrain hinges for stability. Use the House template to cut the felt needle holders.

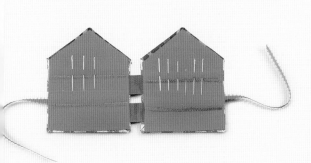

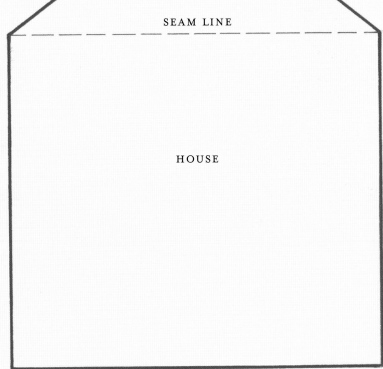

SEAM LINE

HOUSE

Quilt Block Heart Pillow

Betty Auth

ARTIST

ABOUT THE VINTAGE FRAGMENTS

Many creative people share the compulsion to visit flea markets, antique malls, and estate and tag sales. Here they can find inspiration while shopping for vintage materials to add to their stash. Take a close look at this heart pillow and you'll recognize fragments of a Mariner's Compass quilt block. Betty Auth discovered a cache of these blocks in an antique mall somewhere on the road between Texas and Florida. The rounded compass design had potential. In a basket of damaged goods she found a tattered dresser scarf, its intact segments of orange, green, and black embroidery announcing "period piece" loud and clear. The big leaf sequin on the front of the pillow was encapsulated in a plastic sandwich bag along with other odds and ends, and the bargain price for the lot was too tempting to resist.

To design your own heart pillow, search through your stash for a quilt block to serve as the focus of the design. Pieced star patterns are especially suitable for the curved wedge shapes you will need for this project (see the illustrations on page 32). Once you have selected a quilt block, pick out some embroidery fragments and trims to go with it.

VINTAGE FRAGMENTS

- 8" × 8" (20 cm × 20 cm) Mariner's Compass quilt block
- embroidered dresser scarf

MATERIALS

- 14" × 14" (36 cm × 36 cm) velvet or velour (for pillow back)
- 20" × 20" (51 cm × 51 cm) muslin (for base)
- 1 ⅛ yards (1 m) 1"-wide (3 cm) upholstery trim or gimp
- assorted scraps:
  velvet or velour fabrics
  wide silk ribbon
  wide metallic ribbon
- 2" (5 cm) ornamental leaf sequin
- 4mm crystal beads
- seed beads
- pearl cotton or embroidery floss
- sewing thread
- beading thread
- fiberfill
- fabric glue
- fray inhibitor

TOOLS

- sewing machine
- steam iron
- sewing shears
- needles: sharps, embroidery, beading
- straight pins
- 16" (41 cm) quilting hoop
- turning tool
- presscloth
- fabric marking pen
- template-making supplies (see page 12)
- photocopier

T I P : *If a trim is exceptionally prone to* RAVELING, *treat it with a fray inhibitor at the start of your project.*

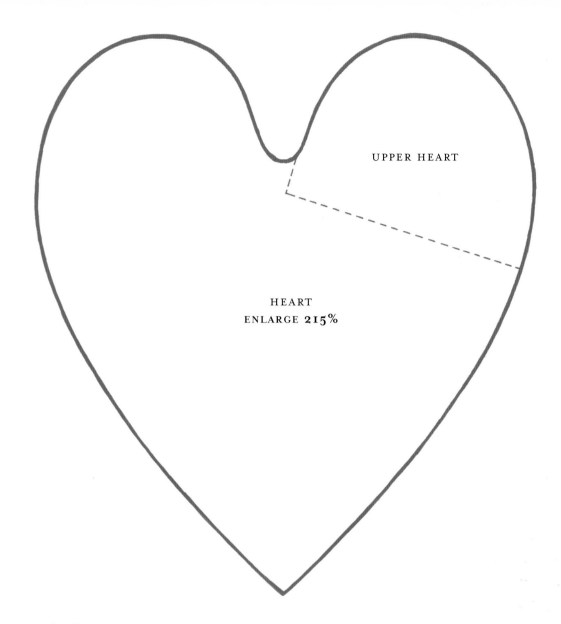

UPPER HEART

HEART
ENLARGE **215%**

INSTRUCTIONS

1. Photocopy the heart pattern (above) at 215%, or so it measures about 11½"
(29 cm) wide. Use the enlarged pattern to make 1 Heart template and 1 Upper
Heart template.

2. Lay the muslin flat. Center the Heart template on the muslin, and trace around the
outline. Secure the marked muslin in the quilting hoop.

3. From the velvet or velour scraps, cut 2 Upper Heart shapes (reverse 1). Place the
shapes on the muslin heart, aligning the curved edges. Select and cut 2 sections
from the embroidered dresser scarf. Place one on each upper heart.

4. Cut a wedge-shaped piece from the Mariner's Compass quilt block. Trim close to the outside points to curve the upper edge. Position the wedge on the middle of the muslin heart. Cut a smaller wedge-shaped piece from the same quilt block to cover the lower part of the heart. Position it on the muslin.

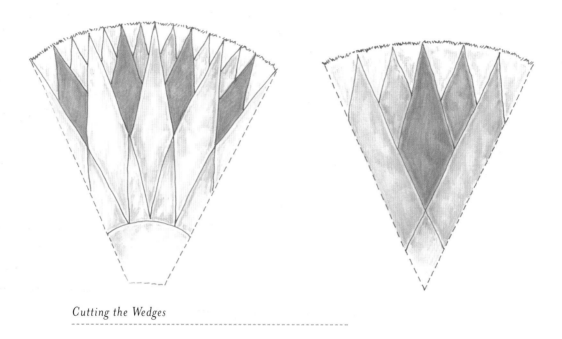

Cutting the Wedges

5. Use the assorted fabric and ribbon scraps to fill out the remaining areas within the heart outline. Let the finished edges of the ribbons overlap and conceal the raw fabric edges by at least ½" (1 cm). If any raw edges remain exposed, treat them with fray inhibitor. When you are satisfied with your arrangement, remove the pieces and set them aside, keeping track of their placement.

6. Position a velour upper heart on the muslin. Hand-baste around the edges with a long running stitch to hold it in place. Add and baste the second velour upper heart in the same way. Continue to add and baste each piece of fabric and ribbon in turn, overlapping the edges (and previous basting stitches) as you go. Check the back of the work occasionally. In addition to various basting lines, a heart-shaped outline should emerge.

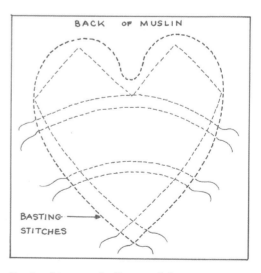

Basting Lines on the Reverse Side

7. Use an embroidery needle threaded with pearl cotton or three strands of floss to work blanket stitch along the edges of some of the ribbons and fabric pieces. Tack down the curved raw edges of the quilt block with matching thread and allow them to fray.

8. Use a beading needle and thread to attach crystal beads and clusters of seed beads to the quilt block where the individual points meet. Sew the leaf sequin to the center front. Treat any remaining raw edges with fray inhibitor or glue on decorative trim to conceal them. Let dry overnight.

9. Remove the muslin from the quilting hoop. Lay the 14" × 14" (36 cm × 36 cm) square of velvet flat, right side up. Place the decorated muslin facedown on top. Pin the pieces together. Machine-stitch ½" (1 cm) inside the heart outline through all layers, leaving a 4" (10 cm) opening for turning. Reinforce the seam by sewing a second line of stitching alongside the first one. Trim the seam allowance to ¼" (0.5 cm). Clip the curves. Turn the pillow cover right side out. Use a turning tool to poke out the point and smooth the curves. Press lightly, using a presscloth. Stuff firmly with fiberfill. Hand-sew the opening closed.

10. Starting on a straight edge, run upholstery trim around the outside edge of the pillow, to conceal the seam. Hand-sew the trim along both edges, using tiny, closely spaced stitches to prevent gaps. When you reach the starting point, fold in the overlapping end, trim off any excess, and tack securely.

> **T I P :** *When you want to use a* **WIRED RIBBON** *for its color but don't need the shape-holding aspect, remove the wire. Grip one end of the wire with small needlenose pliers and pull gently to draw it out.*

Collage Jewelry Box

Judi Kauffman

ARTIST

ABOUT THE VINTAGE FRAGMENTS

Judi Kauffman loves to create collages with old things. She also loves updating the look by mixing in embellishments available today. Her friends and family indulge her passion by passing on the "junque" they accrue when cleaning out drawers and cupboards. Through their largesse, Judi received a doily and a bread tray liner that were damaged by stains and holes but too beautiful to throw away. By adding color and embellishments from her studio stash, she transformed them into an inset for the top of a musical jewelry box.

Since no two people will have collected the same vintage fragments, each collage creation is always unique. Use Judi's box to inspire your own assemblage, or follow her basic design but change the colors to suit your fancy. Mix in new ribbons, some beads, and custom-made sequins for extra pizzazz.

MATERIALS

- 7¼" × 8¼" × 2¾" (18.5 cm × 20.5 cm × 7 cm) music jewelry box with lid inset
- glass dragonfly
- glass seed beads
- brass shank-style buttons
- assorted iridescent Mylar sheets
- tapestry ribbon
- wide silk ribbon
- sewing thread
- quilting thread
- beading thread
- thin quilt batting
- gem glue
- fabric glue
- double-sided tape (optional)

VINTAGE FRAGMENTS

- 7" × 5½" (18 cm × 14 cm) solid textured fabric (for background)
- 4½" (11 cm) round crocheted doily
- lace bread tray liner
- embroidered silk appliqué
- large cameo

TOOLS

- fabric dyes or fabric pens
- butterfly punch
- flower punch
- sewing shears
- needles: sewing, quilting, beading
- straight pins

INSTRUCTIONS

1. Tint the doily and lace bread tray liner with fabric dyes or fabric pens, following the manufacturer's instructions. Use the colors shown (see page 38) or substitute colors of your choice. Let dry.

2. Lay the background fabric flat, right side up. Arrange the doily, lace bread liner, and tapestry ribbon on top in a design that you like. Secure with straight pins. Tack in place with a needle and matching thread.

3. Use a quilting needle and thread to hand-sew a meandering running stitch through the open areas of the background.

4. Cut a 4" to 5" (10 cm to 13 cm) length of wide silk ribbon. Hand-sew a long running stitch along one long edge. Pull the thread from both ends to draw up the gathers. Tie off. Arrange the gathered ribbon, embroidered silk appliqué, cameo, and buttons on the collage. Sew the pieces in place with matching sewing thread, or attach them with fabric glue or gem glue.

> *Before gluing on* BUTTONS, *clip off the shanks. The wire cutter tool on a pair of needlenose pliers is strong enough to cut through most metal shanks.*

5. Use the punches to cut several butterflies and flowers from the assorted Mylar sheets. Layer the butterfly cutouts in pairs. Use a sharp needle to pierce a hole at each end of the butterfly body through both layers. Use a beading needle and thread to sew each layered butterfly to the collage, threading on a few glass seed beads for the body as you go. Pierce a hole in each flower and attach it with a seed bead in the same way. Glue on the glass dragonfly.

6. Place the cardboard insert that comes with the music box on a flat surface. Cut three pieces of thin quilt batting: 6" × 4¼" (15 cm × 10.5 cm), 5" × 3¼" (13 cm × 8.5 cm), and 4" × 2¼" (10 cm × 5.5 cm). Center each piece of batting on the insert, smallest to largest, for the layered padding.

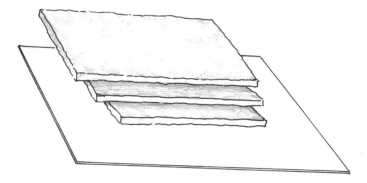

Layer the Batting

7. Place the collage right side up on the batting. Turn over the entire layered sandwich. Fold in the corners diagonally and secure them with fabric glue. Hold in place for a few minutes, or until the glue sets.

8. Fold the edges onto the back of the insert and glue in place. Let dry. Secure the insert in the top of the music box with fabric glue or double-sided tape.

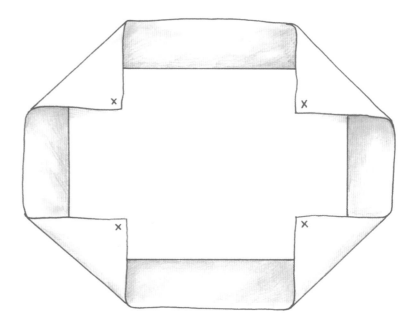

Fold in the Corners

Novelty Fabrics

SHIMMERY SHEERS, ROUGH-TOUGH TEXTURES—
AND IF YOU CAN'T FIND THE FABRIC YOU WANT,
PAINT YOUR OWN!

A Box of Jewels

Lynne Sward

ARTIST

ABOUT THE NOVELTY FABRICS

Gorgeous metallic organzas, shimmery chiffons, and sheer silks come up looking like fine jewels in the hands of designer Lynne Sward. Each of these fabrics is spectacular on its own, but Lynne doesn't stop there. By overlaying various pieces and throwing in lengths of sheer ribbon, she creates a fabric collage with intriguing depth. At last, those bridal, lingerie, and evening wear scraps you've stashed away can find a home.

Metallic threads hold the multiple layers together and lock in the smaller pieces that are trapped inside the sandwich. The machine stitching careens off course so many times, you know this collage has to be fun to sew. When your collage is complete, cut it into strips for a posh bead necklace and a sculptural jewelry box to match.

NOVELTY FABRICS

- printed chiffon
- metallics, especially sheers
- organza
- sheer and metallic ribbons

MATERIALS

- cotton flannel
- plain cotton fabric
- 4 sheets of thin craft foam
- space-dyed chenille yarn
- assorted small glass beads
- assorted metallic threads
- rayon sewing thread
- beading thread

TOOLS

- sewing machine
- sewing shears
- needles: sharps, beading, embroidery
- straight pins
- template-making supplies (see page 12)
- fabric marking pen

INSTRUCTIONS

Making the Sheer Collage

1. Lay the plain cotton fabric over the cotton flannel. Cut a rectangle at least 9" × 11" (23 cm × 28 cm), but larger if possible, through both layers.

2. Layer small pieces of the various chiffon, metallic, and organza fabrics and ribbons on the rectangle. Let the sheer fabrics overlap for two or three layers to create new colors and designs. Overlay the entire collage with a large piece of sheer fabric.

3. Machine-stitch through all the layers using assorted metallic threads and a combination of zigzag and straight stitches. Make the stitching lines overlap and crisscross each other at random to jazz up the collage. Repeat steps 1–3 as needed.

> **TIP:** *Metallic threads tend to slip around during machine sewing. To keep things from spiraling out of control, insert a plastic drinking straw into the spool hole. Then set the spool onto the machine spindle. The straw extension will act as a thread guard.*

Making the Jewelry Box

1. Use the patterns below to make templates A and E. Mark and cut the following shapes from the collaged fabric:

4 A   use template A
2 B   2" × 3½" (5 cm × 9 cm)
4 C   2" × 4¼" (5 cm × 10.5 cm)
4 D   2" × 5¾" (4 cm × 15 cm)
2 E   use template E

2. Mark 2 A, 1 B, 2 C, 2 D, and 1 E on craft foam. Cut out each craft foam piece ¼" (0.5 cm) inside the marked lines all around.

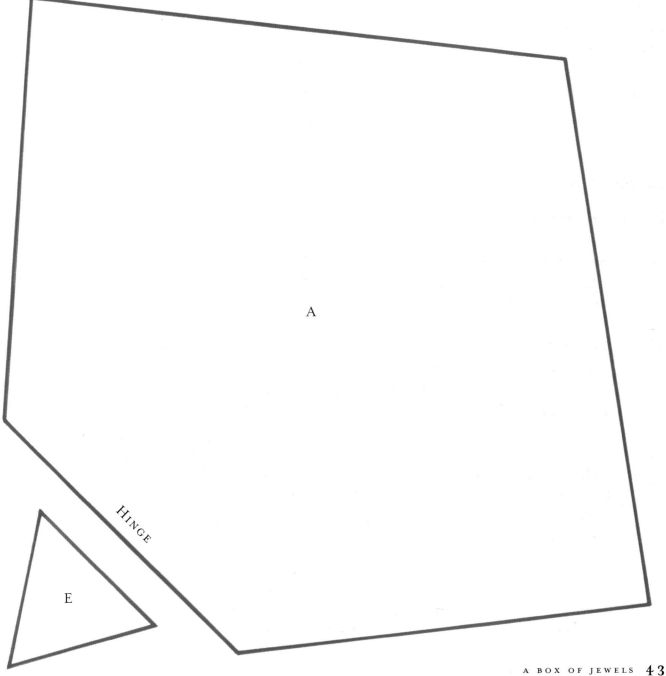

3. Layer 2 fabric collage A's wrong sides together. Sandwich a craft foam A in between. Pin around the edges. Pair up and layer the remaining pieces in the same way. Select one A sandwich for the base of the jewelry box. Trim the outside edges of this sandwich a scant ⅛" (0.3 cm) all around.

4. Set the sewing machine for a closely spaced zigzag stitch. Use coordinating rayon sewing thread to zigzag around the edges of each piece. Zigzag a second time using metallic thread.

5. Pin 1 B, 2 C, and 2 D pieces together end to end in the order shown, for the box sides. Hand-sew using beading thread and a small overcast stitch. Join the D's together and then add base A. Sew the remaining A piece to the top edge of B for a hinged lid. Sew tab E to the top front of the lid.

D	C	B	C	D

The Box Sides

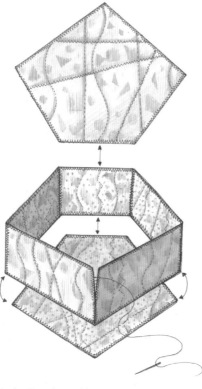

Completing the Box Assembly

Making the Necklace

1. Mark and cut six short strips from the collaged fabric:

A   1¾" (5 cm) wide   D   1⅜" (4 cm) wide

B   1⅝" (4.5 cm) wide   E   1¼" (3.5 cm) wide

C   1½" (4 cm) wide   F   1⅛" (3.3 cm) wide

2. Cut each strip into 2" (5 cm) segments. The necklace shown uses these segments: 3 A, 2 B, 3 C, 2 D, 1 E, and 1 F.

3. Set the sewing machine for a closely spaced zigzag stitch. Using rayon or metallic thread, zigzag the 2" (5 cm) edges and a third edge of each segment. Leave the fourth edge unstitched.

Zigzag Three Edges

4. Starting with the unstitched edge, roll each segment into a tight cylindrical bead. Secure with a pin. Overcast the overlapping edge and ends by hand to secure the roll. Use a beading needle and thread to embellish the surface with randomly placed glass seed beads.

Roll into a Bead

5. For the pendant, arrange an A, a C, and an F bead in a graduated horizontal stack. Use a sharps needle and beading thread to sew the beads together. Add bead E, vertically placed, to the bottom of F.

6. Thread a large embroidery needle with three 35" (89 cm) lengths of chenille yarn. Thread the rolled beads onto the yarn strands in the following order: A, B, C, D, D, C, B, A, and pendant bead A. Remove the needle. Knot the yarn ends together and clip off the excess. Slide the pendant bead A over the knot. Adjust the remaining beads so that there is about 9" (23 cm) between the two D beads and 1" (3 cm) between the others.

7. Thread a beading needle with beading thread, but do not cut the thread from the spool. Starting at the pendant, draw the beading thread through the rolled beads, slipping small glass beads onto the exposed sections as you go. When you reach the starting point, draw the thread through the A bead and knot off. Tack a few loose strands of beads to the bottom of the pendant and let them dangle down.

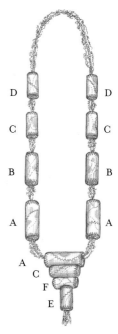

Necklace Assembly

Footstool Slipcover

Pat Claus

ARTIST

ABOUT THE NOVELTY FABRICS

A peony as big as a cabbage? When you paint it yourself, any design is possible. This fantastic floral specimen by Pat Claus is colored with fabric paints. In the background, pools of blue, green, and violet intermingle—another example of Pat's color artistry. The painting is not especially difficult. First, design holding lines are traced onto the fabric with a permanent pen. Wetting the fabric before applying the paint encourages the colors to spread. When two colors touch, they blend together effortlessly, sometimes surprising even the artist with their lush combinations.

Streaks of white opaque paint overlay the petals, but the real definition comes from the quilting. Each petal is outlined with machine stitching that adds three-dimensional beauty. The painted and quilted flower can be used in a variety of ways—for a pillow, a tote, wall art, or the fun footstool slipcover shown here.

Machine quilting by Barb Knoblock.

NOVELTY FABRICS

- 1 yard (0.9 m) white cotton fabric
- fabric paints:
    - cobalt blue
    - fuchsia
    - buttercup
    - orange
    - ultramarine
    - green
    - violet
    - turquoise
    - white opaque

MATERIALS

- rectangular upholstered footstool
- ½ to 1 yard (0.45 m to 0.9 m) coordinating fabric (for ruffle)
- ½ to 1 yard (0.45 m to 0.9 m) muslin
- batting
- sewing thread
- small glass beads or fabric glitter
- fabric glue

TOOLS

- sewing machine
- steam iron
- photocopier
- sewing shears
- straight pins
- tape measure
- fine-tip and heavy-tip black permanent markers
- dressmaker's chalk
- sea sponge
- pointed round liner brush
- masking tape
- scissors
- ruler
- pencil and paper
- large plastic sheet

INSTRUCTIONS

Painting the Fabric

I. Measure the width, length, and height (W, L, H) of the footstool. Jot down your figures. Enlarge the flower pattern (page 49) on a photocopier to the desired size. The flower can fill out the top of the stool only or some petals can spill down onto the sides.

2. Machine-wash the white fabric to remove the manufacturer's sizing; do not use fabric softener in the rinse. Dry the fabric and iron out the wrinkles. Use chalk and a ruler to mark a rectangle that measures W × L on the middle of the fabric. Measure 5" (13 cm) beyond the rectangle all around and mark a second rectangle. Cut on the outside line.

Flower Pattern. Enlarge to desired size.

3. Tape the enlarged pattern to a flat work surface. Lay the fabric on top, with the flower design centered, and tape down. If you cannot see the design lines through the fabric, tape both pieces to a large window instead. Use a fine-tip permanent marker to trace the flower design lines.

4. Smooth the fabric over a large work surface protected with plastic. Tape down the edges so that the fabric is taut and wrinkle-free.

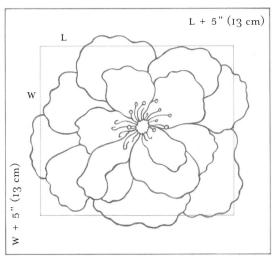

Mark the Design

5. Brush clear water onto one petal, staying at least ¼" (0.5 cm) within the marked outline. Dip the brush into fuchsia paint and touch it lightly to the wet fabric in several spots. Allow the color to bleed out in several directions. Rinse out the brush. Repeat this technique to add buttercup, orange, ultramarine, and violet to the petal. Rinse the brush between colors. Try to give each color its own space. Repeat until each petal is filled. At the center of the flower, apply buttercup paint. Let dry.

6. Repeat the step 5 technique to paint the background. Wet the fabric and then apply cobalt blue, ultramarine, emerald green, violet, and turquoise. Let dry.

7. Use a sea sponge to lightly dab violet paint over the background. Use a brush to apply several dots of violet paint to the center of the flower for the stamens. Rinse the brush and load it with white opaque paint. Starting at the outside edge of a petal, pull the brush toward the center to make a white streak. Repeat around the entire petal edge, reloading the brush often, to create white highlights. Do this for each petal. Let dry.

Sewing the Slipcover

1. Cut a muslin rectangle and a batting rectangle, both slightly larger than your painted piece. Layer all three pieces for quilting, with the painted flower on top. Machine-quilt along the petal edges. Quilt short lines for the stamens. Use a meandering or stippling stitch in the background. Trim off the excess batting and muslin.

2. Center the quilted flower facedown on the footstool. Fold each corner diagonally, pinching to take up the excess, and pin. Stitch along the pinned lines to box the corners. Trim ¼" (0.5 cm) beyond the stitching lines.

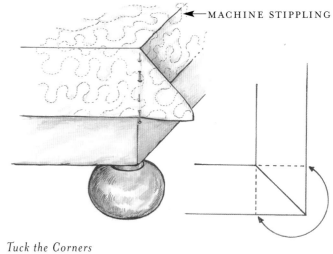

←MACHINE STIPPLING

Tuck the Corners

3. Put the painted flower faceup on the footstool. Measure around the stool to find the perimeter (P). For the ruffle drop (D), measure down from the raw edge of the flower piece to the desired hem length, and add ½" (1 cm) for the seam allowance. The ruffle on the project footstool stops about 1" (3 cm) from the floor. Jot down your figures for P and D.

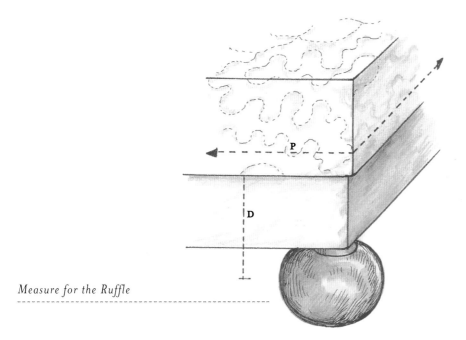

Measure for the Ruffle

4. Multiply P × 2 and add 1" (3 cm) for the ruffle length. Multiply D × 2 and add 2" (5 cm) for the ruffle width. Cut the ruffle fabric to these dimensions. You may have to join several pieces together to obtain a strip that is the required length.

5. To attach the ruffle, bring the ends of the ruffle strip right sides together and stitch. Press the seam open. Fold the ruffle lengthwise in half, wrong side in, and press. Machine-baste ⅜" (1 cm) and ⅝" (1.5 cm) from the raw edges all around. Pull the lower threads simultaneously to draw up the gathers. Adjust the gathers to match the P measurement. Pin the ruffle to the lower edge of the flower piece, right sides together. Stitch with a ½" (1 cm) seam allowance.

6. Glue small glass beads or glitter to the center of the flower for the pistils. Let dry.

Crazy Quilt Silk Bags

Valerie Fontenot

ARTIST

ABOUT THE NOVELTY FABRICS

Valerie Fontenot is Betty Auth's daughter. Mother and daughter often worked side by side, drawing from Betty's rich stash, to create unique projects. These retro-look purses are a result of their collaboration. Each purse is sewn from raw silk shantung and adorned with vintage drapery and upholstery fabrics. The classy barkcloths and printed chintzes attest to Betty's keen eye for tag sale bargains.

You can decorate these shoulder-sling purses with as much or as little orna-mentation as you wish. On the pale pink bag, the crazy-patch runs from the foldover flap onto the purse back. On the champagne bag, only the flap is decorated. Chunky pearl cotton embroidery, plastic and glass beads, and novelty buttons play along with the fabrics, teasing out the color highlights. The short front flap makes it easy to add your own edge treatment.

NOVELTY FABRICS

- retro decorator fabrics, including barkcloth and chintz
- handkerchiefs with embroidered corners
- lace trim

MATERIALS

- ¼ yard (0.23 m) raw silk shantung
- scrap of taffeta (for lining)
- scrap of muslin (for foundation)
- assorted glass and plastic beads
- assorted buttons
- 6" (15 cm) length of rayon fringe
- 1 ¼ yards (1.1 m) narrow twisted cord
- pearl cotton, assorted
- cotton and silk sewing threads

TOOLS

- sewing machine
- steam iron
- sewing shears
- needles: sharps, embroidery, beading
- straight pins
- fabric marking pen
- ruler

Instructions

I. Mark and cut three fabric pieces:

A   7" × 16½" (18 cm × 42 cm) silk shantung
B   7" × 7½" (18 cm × 19 cm) silk shantung
C   7" × 12" (18 cm × 30 cm) taffeta

2. Machine-stitch A to C, right sides together, along one 7" (18 cm) edge. Press the seam allowance toward A. At the other end of A, baste a 7" (18 cm) length of fringe.

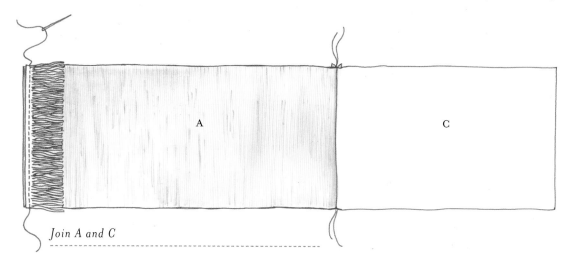

Join A and C

3. Fold one 7" (18 cm) edge of B ½" (1 cm) to the wrong side and press. Fold in the same edge another ½" (1 cm) and press. To form the pocket, place B on A, right sides together and raw edges matching. Machine-stitch around three sides with a ½" (1 cm) seam allowance, enclosing the fringe in the seam. Trim out the excess.

4. To form the lining, fold C back on itself, right side in, so that the raw edge extends ½" (1 cm) beyond the seam line. Stitch the raw edges together, starting at the seam line and using a ½" (1 cm) seam allowance. Stitch again ⅛" (0.3 cm) in from the previous stitching (a ⅝" [1.5 cm] seam allowance).

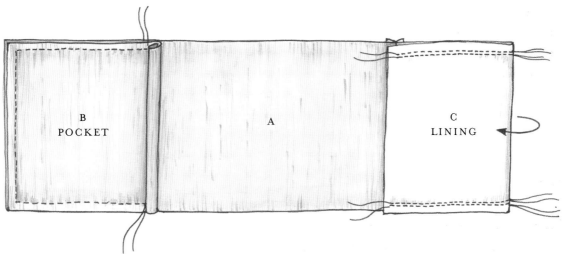

Make the Pocket and Lining

5. To form the flap, fold C onto B so that the fold line of C almost meets the stitching line of B. Starting about 1" (3 cm) from the lining seam, stitch the raw edges of A together using a ½" (1 cm) seam allowance.

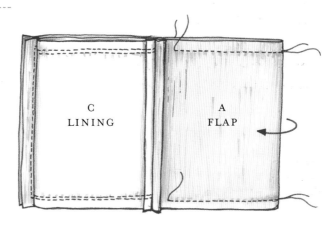

Form the Flap

6. Use sewing shears to trim the lining seam allowance close to the first stitching line. Trim the remaining seam allowances to ¼" (0.5 cm). Trim the corners diagonally. Turn the pocket and the flap right side out and poke out the corners. Press well. Tuck the lining into the pocket. (It will be hand-tacked later.)

7. Decide whether to crazy-patch all of piece A or just the flap portion. Draw this shape on muslin. Cut out the muslin 1" (3 cm) beyond the marked line all around.

8. Use the crazy-patch technique (see page 15) to apply the assorted barkcloth, chintz, and decorator fabrics to the muslin foundation. Go out beyond the marked lines until the muslin is filled. Trim out the excess bulk, including the muslin, wherever possible. Pin the crazy-patch collage to the purse. Trim the allowance to about ⅜" (1 cm), or a width you can comfortably turn under. Add a trim (see the box below) to the lower edge of the flap, if desired. Slipstitch the crazy-patch in place, turning under the edges and removing the pins as you go.

9. Use pearl cotton to embroider assorted decorative stitches over the crazy-patch seams. Stitch through the crazy-patch fabrics only; be careful not to pierce the facing fabrics. (A piece of stiff plastic or cardboard slipped into the pocket can act as a needle shield.) The stitches used include straight stitch, blanket stitch, chain stitch, chevron stitch, featherstitch, open cretan stitch, and open chain stitch. Tack on buttons and beads to complete your collage.

Some edge trim ideas:
- *a short length of crocheted, tatted, or machine-made lace*
- *a semicircle cut from a doily*
- *one or more embroidered corners from vintage handkerchiefs or napkins*
- *white eyelet trim with ribbon insertion*

10. Open the purse flat. Knot each end of the twisted cord. Tuck a knotted end into each side seam, just above the lining. Slipstitch closed. Slipstitch the lining to the inside of the purse pocket.

Old Fancies

Fabrics and trims with a Victorian pedigree,
real or imagined.

Velvet Pincushions

Gretchen Nutt

ARTIST

ABOUT THE OLD FANCIES

This trio of pincushions only looks antique. The secret behind the vintage appearance is the hand-dyed silk ribbons and silk/rayon velvets. Artist Gretchen Nutt brushes the dye colors onto the damp fibers, achieving subtle gradations and blends that are not possible when the fabric is dipped all at once. A lovely texture results if the fabric is crinkled and then laid flat to dry.

Once the dyeing is complete, Gretchen brings multiple colors together in each pincushion. Her silk ribbon embroidery includes yellow climbing roses, magenta hollyhocks with translucent glass beads, and hostas with splendidly large leaves. Silk buttonhole twist embroidery continues the color play over the seams and back, making each piece a stitch archive you'll want to pick up and study again and again. The elongated triangular shape is comfortable to handle. The sawdust stuffing is ultra-firm and holds pins secure.

OLD FANCIES

- four white 6½" × 11" (17 cm × 28 cm) rectangles silk/rayon velvet (for dyeing)
- white silk ribbon (for dyeing):
  7 yards (6.4 m) 13mm
  4 yards (3.7 m) 7mm
  5 yards (4.6 m) 4mm
- heat-set liquid fabric dyes:
  green
  rose
  yellow
  periwinkle
  red
- antique enameled butterfly pins

MATERIALS

- 40 to 45 Czech pressed glass drop beads
- silk buttonhole twist on 20-meter cards:
  medium yellowish green
  dark yellowish green
  dark periwinkle blue
  magenta
  lavender
  bright yellow
- three 6½" × 11" (17 cm × 28 cm) rectangles craft felt
- sewing thread
- Nymo thread
- very fine sawdust or unprocessed wheat bran

TOOLS

For dyeing:
- 11" × 14" (28 cm × 36 cm) glass baking dish
- assorted brushes
- latex gloves
- old, clean towels
- paper towels
- container of water
- large plastic sheets
- newspapers and/or drop cloths
- steam iron

For sewing:
- sewing machine
- needles: sharps, beading, chenille (sizes 18 and 22)
- sewing shears
- small, sharp embroidery scissors
- fabric marking pen
- ruler
- turning tool

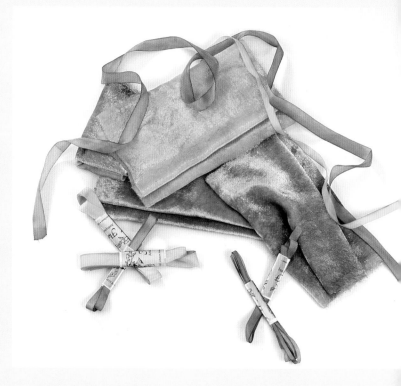

INSTRUCTIONS

Dyeing the Velvet and Ribbons

1. Choose a work area that has ample space for your materials and a spot to dry the finished pieces. Protect the work surface and floor with plastic sheets topped with newspapers or drop cloths. Set out old, clean towels where you can lay your dyed velvets flat for drying. Set up a clothesline for drying ribbons. Wear old clothes and latex gloves.

2. Wet the velvet rectangles with water. Squeeze out the excess moisture. Lay a piece of damp velvet flat in the baking dish. Use a paintbrush to apply liquid dye to the fabric, adding as much or as little color as you wish.

> **TIP** : *Never mix dyes and foods. Reserve your glass baking dish for* DYE PROJECTS ONLY. *Once you have used a container for dyeing, you should never use it again for cooking, serving, or storing food.*

3. Brush on a second color to add highlights and create interesting blends. A dash of rose on yellow, for example, will fan out and dissipate, creating peachy tones. Experiment with different combinations. Use a small brush for more control over the color placement. For more random blending, crumple up the dyed silk and squeeze it. When you are happy with the colors, lay the velvet flat to dry.

4. Repeat steps 2, 3, and 4 to dye all four rectangles. To make three pincushions as shown, you will need 1 rose, 1 yellow-peach, 1 green, and 1 periwinkle rectangle.

5. Cut the white silk ribbons into 1- or 2-yard (0.9 m or 1.8 m) lengths and dampen them. Use the same brush technique to apply the dyes. Hang each ribbon by one end to dry. To make the projects shown, you will need:
5 yards (4.6 m) 13mm green
2 yards (1.8 m) 13mm rose
4 yards (3.7 m) 7mm yellow with red along one edge
3 yards (2.7 m) 4mm lavender
2 yards (1.8 m) 4mm green

6. Use an iron to heat-set the dyes, following the manufacturer's instructions. Protect the ironing board with an old, clean towel, as the dyes may bleed. Let the velvet reach a damp-dry state and then press it from the wrong side. Let the ribbons dry completely and then steam-press lightly.

Making the Pincushions

I. Layer two velvet rectangles right sides together. Use a ruler and a fabric marking pen to draw a diagonal line connecting two opposite corners. Cut on the marked line through both layers. Layer, mark, and cut the two remaining velvet rectangles in the same way. Swap some of the triangles to make three different color pairs: periwinkle/yellow-peach, periwinkle/green, and rose/yellow-peach. (You will have two triangles left over.) Layer each pair right sides together.

2. Mark three felt rectangles on the diagonal. Cut into six triangles. Sandwich each pair of velvet triangles between two felt triangles, matching the edges. Machine-stitch ½" (1 cm) from the edge all around through all the layers. Trim the seam allowance to ¼" (0.5 cm). Clip the corners.

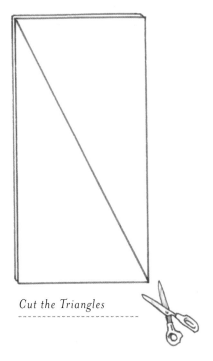

Cut the Triangles

3. Using small, sharp embroidery scissors, cut a slit through one felt layer of each piece. Carefully cut a corresponding slit in the velvet layer immediately under it. Turn the piece right side out through the openings. Poke out the corners with a turning tool.

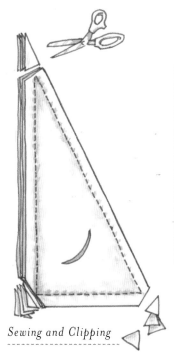

Sewing and Clipping

TIP : CUT YOUR SLIT *according to the embroidery you are planning. In the* HOSTA *design, the slit is in front and is hidden by a rose ribbon. In the* HOLLYHOCKS *and* ROSES *designs, the slits are on the back and are camouflaged with silk buttonhole twist embroidery.*

4. Fill the pincushion with sawdust or wheat bran, pushing it into the corners and packing firmly. Hand-sew the felt opening closed. Then sew up the velvet opening.

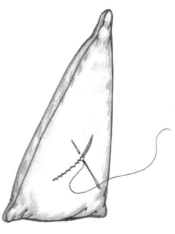

Stuff and Sew Closed

Roses Embellishment

Use a periwinkle/yellow-peach pincushion.

- On the periwinkle velvet side, work rambling **feather-stitch** vines in yellowish green silk buttonhole twist.

- Use 7mm yellow ribbon to load the vines with **spiderweb** roses and **ribbon stitch** buds. The red edge will help create the illusion of petals.

- Use 4mm green ribbon to add **ribbon stitch** leaves at the bases of the roses and buds.

- Continue the rambling **featherstitch** vine onto the yellow-peach side and around the outside seam. Run one part of the vine directly over the closed seam opening to camouflage it. Use periwinkle and bright yellow silk buttonhole twist to add **lazy daisy** buds.

- Pin an **antique butterfly** pin to the front of the pincushion.

Hollyhocks Embellishment

Use a green/periwinkle pincushion.

- -

- On the green velvet side, begin the hollyhocks at the top and work down. Using dark yellowish green silk buttonhole twist, work **straight stitch** stems, curving them as you reach the base of the triangle. Add a few tight **French knots** for buds at the top of each stem.

- For the flowers, use 13mm rose silk ribbon. Embroider loopy **straight stitches** down each stem, graduating the sizes so that the loops grow larger as you near the bottom. Tack down the loops with **Czech pressed glass drop beads**.

- Work the leaves in **ribbon stitch** with 13mm green silk ribbon. Concentrate the leaves near the base, but add a few along the upper stems as well.

- Continue the rambling **featherstitch** vine onto the periwinkle side and around the outside seam. Run one part of the vine directly over the closed seam opening to camouflage it. Use magenta silk buttonhole twist to add **lazy daisy** buds.

Hosta Embellishment

Use a rose/yellow-peach pincushion.

- On the rose velvet side, conceal the slit opening with a long straight stitch of 13mm rose silk ribbon.

- For the hosta leaves, embroider two generous clumps of **ribbon stitch** with green 13mm silk ribbon.

- For the flowers, make long **straight stitch** stems in yellow-ish green silk buttonhole twist. Then use lavender 4mm silk ribbon to work ribbon stitch along the stems.

- Use yellowish green silk buttonhole twist to work a rambling **featherstitch** vine on the yellow-peach velvet and around the outside seam. Add **lazy daisy** buds to the vines with buttonhole twist, using magenta around the outside seam and lavender on the back.

- Pin an antique butterfly pin to the front of the pincushion.

Silk Brocade Purse

Carla J. Peery

ARTIST

ABOUT THE OLD FANCIES

Silk brocade is pure luxury, as is this purse by Carla J. Peery. Delicate quilting stitches, hand-sewn with the finest silk thread, accent the shimmering surface design and make the lightly padded layers puff out ever so slightly. Glittery excitement comes with the hand-sewn Japanese rocaille beads, which trace the brocade pattern, and a beaded loop fringe. The lining is silk faille.

If your stash doesn't include pieces of a vintage silk dressing gown or boudoir pillow to work from, don't worry. It's easy enough to "age" a modern textile with dye. A gorgeous version can also be made with velvet, taffeta, or moiré. If this is your first attempt at making a purse to fit a metal frame, you may be more comfortable using one of these more affordable substitutes.

OLD FANCIES

- new or vintage 5½" (14 cm) gold finish Victorian purse frame
- 18" (46 cm) length of gold-filled chain for handle
- ³/₈ yard (0.4 m) new or vintage silk brocade
- ³/₈ yard (0.4 m) pale pink silk faille (for lining)
- silk fabric dye (optional)

MATERIALS

- ¼ yard (0.23 m) muslin, prewashed and ironed
- ¼ yard (0.23 m) low-loft cotton batting
- silk sewing thread
- ³/₄ yard (0.7 m) pink narrow braid trim
- Japanese seed beads, pale green, size 11/0
- three 36" (91 cm) lengths of pale pink, silver-lined seed beads, size 10/0
- silk quilting thread
- clear (white) beading thread

TOOLS

- sewing machine
- steam iron
- sewing shears
- needles: sharps (size 10), beading
- silk straight pins
- tape measure
- template-making supplies (see page 12)
- pencil
- ruler

INSTRUCTIONS
Preparing the Fabrics

I. To give new silk brocade an aged look, use silk fabric dye and follow the manufacturer's dyeing instructions. Test the color on a small swatch first.

2. To make the templates, lay a sheet of plain paper flat. Place the purse frame near the top edge of the paper. Trace the inside contour with a pencil. Use a pencil and ruler to draw a rectangle directly below the contoured line. Mark an X on each side of the panel where the frame ends. Draw a 1½"-wide (4 cm) gusset panel at each side. Trace the panel and gusset onto template plastic, adding ¼" (0.5 cm) all around both shapes for seam allowances. Cut out both templates.

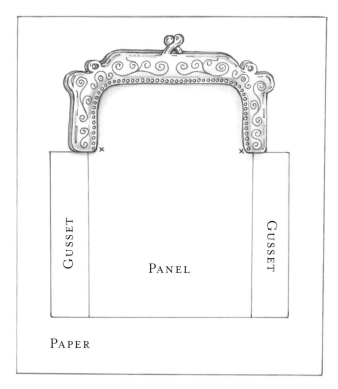

GUSSET

GUSSET

PANEL

PAPER

Make a Template

3. Use the templates to cut 2 panels and 2 gussets from the silk brocade and 2 panels from the lining. Also cut 2 panels each from the batting and muslin, adding an extra 1" (3 cm) all around to allow for the quilting take-up.

Making the Purse

1. Layer the two lining panels right sides together. Using silk sewing thread, machine-stitch around three sides, between the X's, with a ½" (1 cm) seam allowance. Press the remaining raw edges ½" (1 cm) to the wrong side. Turn the lining wrong side out, or as it will fall when inside the purse.

2. Layer a muslin, a batting, and a silk brocade panel together, with the silk brocade right side up on top. Pin lightly on each edge. Baste ¼" (0.5 cm) from the edge of the silk brocade all around. Remove the pins.

3. Refer to Beading on page 16 to embellish the panel with hand beading. Use a #10 sharps needle and clear bead thread to sew on the beads through all three layers. In the featured project, green and pink seed beads accentuate the brocade's vine-and-flower design. Keep the beading about 1" (3 cm) away from the outside edges so that the beads won't get caught in the seams.

4. Use a quilting needle and silk quilting thread to hand-quilt areas that are not beaded. Once again, the design lines in the fabric can provide a path for your stitching. The quilted panel should feel very soft and lightly padded.

TIP: *Silk brocade's* WOVEN-IN DESIGN *makes embellishing easy. You can follow the lines woven into the fabric to add beads and hand quilting.*

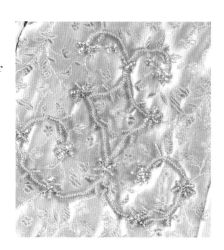

5. Trim the excess batting and muslin even with the silk brocade. Remove the basting stitches. Repeat steps 2–5 to make the second panel. If you wish, you can skip step 3 and simply quilt the second panel.

6. Pin the gussets to one quilted panel, right sides together. Machine-stitch, stopping ¼" (0.5 cm) from each X. Press the seams open. Join and press the remaining panel in the same way. At the top of the purse, fold all the raw edges ¼" (0.5 cm) to the wrong side. Hand-baste the fold on each gusset.

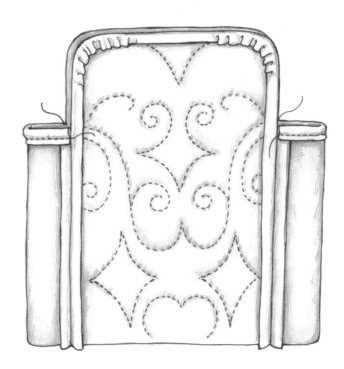

Assemble the Pieces

Lay the purse flat, wrong side out. Tuck in each gusset as shown. Stitch straight across the bottom through all layers. Turn right side out.

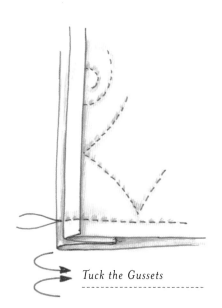

Tuck the Gussets

7. Using a sharps needle and silk thread, hand-sew the purse to the frame. Take very small stitches, running the thread through every stitching hole on the frame. Trim off the excess fabric on the inside to reduce bulk. Insert the lining, still wrong side out, into the purse. Hand-sew it to the frame. Sew narrow braid trim to the lining to conceal the frame stitching. If you wish, trim the outside of the purse as well.

8. For the beaded loop fringe, pour some pink seed beads into a flat bowl. Thread a beading needle with 18" (46 cm) of silk quilting thread. Knot one end. Take a small hidden stitch at one bottom corner of the purse. Dip into the beads with the tip of the needle, picking up several at a time, until you have about 3" (8 cm) of beads on the thread. Take another small stitch very close to the first one. Pull up snugly, forming a bead loop about 1½" (4 cm) long, and take a small holding stitch.

9. Make a new stitch next to the loop you just completed. String on more beads, make a second beaded loop, and secure it. Continue adding beaded loops across the bottom of the purse, rethreading the needle between loops as necessary. End off with a small stitch and a hidden knot. Attach chain to purse frame.

T I P : *The thread on prestrung seed beads is for temporary use only. To make a loop fringe, you'll need to restring the beads on stronger thread.*

Silk and Satin Bottle Covers

Dee Stark

ARTIST

ABOUT THE OLD FANCIES

According to Dee Stark, some fabrics merely "speak" to her while others "sing in her key." Dee loves seeking out simpatico pieces at estate sales and online auctions and confesses to casting a lustful eye on "strange men wearing fabulous ties." When her stash reached a critical mass, it began acting like a magnet, drawing in yet more contributions from family and friends.

Dee dipped into her bottomless stash to create these luscious bottle covers. In the bathroom or on a vanity, where you might have a conglomeration of lotion and cologne bottles, covers like these can give everything a together look. Old threads, ribbons, beads, and trims are layered over silk and satin fabrics to create an amazing display of colors and patterns. While it isn't necessary to use this many different crazy quilt stitches to produce a lush effect, sometimes you just can't help going over the top.

OLD FANCIES

- assorted vintage silks, satins, jacquards, and velvets
- assorted buttons and beads
- assorted decorative embroidery threads
- assorted trims

MATERIALS (FOR ONE COVER)

- 1 fat quarter cotton print theme fabric
- ⅓ yard (0.3 m) muslin, prewashed
- ¾ yard (0.7 m) of ⅛" (0.3 cm) piping filler cord (optional)
- neutral sewing thread

TOOLS

- sewing machine
- sewing shears
- needles: sharps, embroidery, quilting, beading
- fabric marking pen
- template-making supplies (see page 12)
- tape measure
- scissors
- saucer

INSTRUCTIONS

1. Use a tape measure to measure up and around the bottle (an upside-down U shape). Add 2" (5 cm) to allow for ease and seams and divide by 2. Jot down your result and label it H. Measure around the widest part of the bottle, add 2" (5 cm), and divide by 2. Jot down your result and label it W.

2. Use a ruler and pencil to draw a rectangle that measures H × W on template plastic. Use the rim of a saucer as a template to round off the top two corners. Cut out the template with scissors.

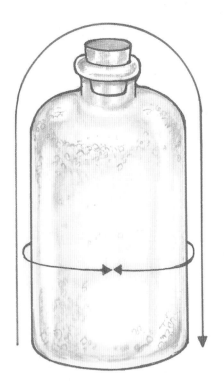

Measure the Bottle

3. Use the template and a fabric marking pen to mark two shapes on muslin. Cut out each shape at least 1" (3 cm) beyond the marked line all around. From the theme print, mark and cut out two template shapes for the lining and one 1½" × 24" (4 cm × 61 cm) strip for the binding.

4. Use the crazy-patch technique (see page 15) to apply the assorted silks, satins, jacquards, and velvets and a few small pieces of your theme fabric to each muslin foundation. Go out beyond the marked lines until each muslin is filled.

5. Turn each piece facedown. Lay the template on the muslin side and trace the outline. Hand-baste just inside the marked line through all the layers. Embellish the seams within the basted outline with assorted embroidery threads, trims, beads, and buttons. Refer to the Embellishment Sampler on page 17 for ideas. Be careful not to place beads, buttons, or French knots too close to the basting line. When you are finished embellishing, use the template to check for shrinkage. Redraw the outline, if necessary, and cut out both shapes.

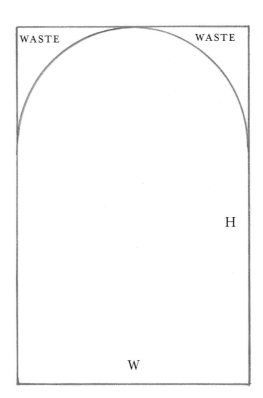

Make a Template

6. Place the two lining pieces right sides together. Place the two crazy-patch pieces right sides together on top of the linings. Pin to hold the layers together. Machine-stitch around the curved edge, making a ½" (1 cm) seam allowance; leave the short straight edge open. Trim the seam allowance to ¼" (0.5 cm), and clip the curves. Turn right side out, letting the lining fall to the inside. Bind the raw edges.

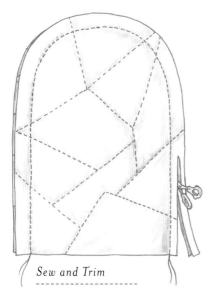

Sew and Trim

Piping Trim

To accentuate a seam line, try narrow piping. For less bulk, sew the lining and outside pieces separately. Then fit the lining inside the cover and bind the raw edges together.

- Cut a bias strip 2" (5 cm) wide and a few inches longer than the seam to be piped.

- Fold the strip in half lengthwise, right side out. Slip a ⅛"-diameter (0.3 cm) piping cord into the fold. Use a zipper foot to stitch close to the cord, but without crowding it.

- Baste the piping to the right side of the project piece, matching the raw edges. You'll find that the bias cut adapts nicely along curves.

- Sew the project pieces together with a zipper foot to enclose the piping in the seam.

Photo Transfers

FAMILIAR FACES PRINTED ON FABRIC—
WHAT MORE COULD A COLLAGE ARTIST WANT?

Accordian-Fold Memory Book

Linda Wyszynski

ARTIST

ABOUT THE PHOTO TRANSFERS

A cloth memory book lets you reach out and touch the past. Fiber artist Linda Wyszynski used photo transfer to reproduce lovely old retouched photos from her husband's family. Her simple accordian-fold design, sewn by Annette Calhoun, tells the romantic story of a young couple who married and journeyed from Poland to America in 1911. A journal excerpt, bits of lace, shell buttons, and a crazy-quilt cover help to set the nostalgic mood. Lightly padded muslin pages, reminiscent of a baby's cloth book, bring their own tactile pleasure to this adult sojourn back in time.

The fold-out section has room for up to twelve images or mini collages. Linda filled six pages and left the reverse side of her accordian foldout blank. If your stash of family ephemera is particularly large, you can work your designs on both sides. The photo transfers are printed on special inkjet-friendly fabric that you run right through your computer printer.

Finishing by Annette Calhoun.

PHOTO TRANSFERS

- two 8½" × 11" (22 cm × 28 cm) sheets of inkjet-printable cotton fabric
- black-and-white family photographs
- diary excerpt or annotation
- map of country of origin

MATERIALS

- ¼ yard (0.23 m) printed cotton fabric, medium to dark value
- coordinating cotton scraps, assorted values (for crazy-patch)
- 1/2 yard (0.45 m) unbleached fine-quality muslin, prewashed and ironed
- ½ yard (0.45 m) fusible interfacing
- ½ yard (0.45 m) thin cotton batting
- sewing thread to match fabrics
- very fine gold braid, size #4
- ecru embroidery floss
- 1"-wide (3 cm) lace with ribbon insertion
- ³/₈"-wide (1 cm) ecru cotton lace edging
- three ½" (1 cm) mother-of-pearl flower buttons
- four ½" (1 cm) natural shell buttons
- black iridescent bugle beads
- dark iridescent seed beads
- fabric glue
- lightweight acid-free cardboard

TOOLS

- sewing machine
- steam iron
- sewing shears
- computer with inkjet printer
- photocopier (optional)
- needles: embroidery, beading, sharps
- straight pins
- water-erasable fabric marker
- ruler or straightedge
- fine-tip permanent marker
- copier paper
- lined notebook paper

INSTRUCTIONS

Making the Transfers

1. Using a computer or photocopier, resize your selected photographs, maps, etc., to 2¾" × 4" (7 cm × 10 cm) or smaller. To simplify a map image, use your computer software or lay a sheet of copier paper over the map and trace the outline by hand with a fine-tip marker. Add a star to represent a key city or region. For a hand-written annotation, draw a 2¾" × 4" (7 cm × 10 cm) rectangle on lined paper, lay plain paper on top, and write your message within the guidelines. The project shown features 3 photos, 1 map, and 1 annotation.

2. Following the manufacturer's instructions, use a computer printer to print your step 1 images onto the special transfer fabric. Group several images on one sheet, allowing at least 1" (3 cm) between images. Allow the ink to dry for several hours, or as the manufacturer recommends.

3. Rinse the images in cool water. Lay them flat and allow to air-dry overnight. Follow the manufacturer's

> **TIP :** *Prepare the photo transfers* FIRST *and set them out to dry while you work on other parts of the project.*

recommendations regarding ironing. Cut the images apart, but do not cut them out.

Making the Crazy Quilt Cover

1. From the cotton print, cut a 6¾" × 8" (17 cm × 20 cm) rectangle and a random five-sided shape, 3" to 5" (8 cm to 13 cm) across. From the muslin, cut a 6" × 8" (15 cm × 20 cm) rectangle.

2. Referring to Crazy-Patch on page 15, cover the 6" × 8" (15 cm × 20 cm) muslin rectangle with crazy quilting. Start at the center with the printed five-sided shape. Add the assorted cottons until the entire muslin rectangle is filled.

3. Turn the work over and trim the excess fabric even with the muslin edge. Baste ¼" (0.5 cm) from the edge all around to stabilize the foundation piecing.

4. On the right side, embellish each crazy-patch seam with very fine gold braid and beads. Hand-sew flower buttons to three of the crazy-patch shapes.

> *Try these Embroidery and Bead Combinations*
> • *gold braid* STEM STITCH *with dark iridescent bugle bead "leaves"*
> • *gold braid* FEATHERSTITCH *with dark iridescent seed bead "buds"*

5. Place the crazy-patch piece and the cotton print rectangle right sides together. Stitch along one 8" (20 cm) edge, making a ½" (1 cm) seam. Press the seam allowance toward the cotton print. Trim as needed to measure 8" × 11¾" (20 cm × 30 cm).

Making the Accordian-Fold Pages

1. From the muslin, cut two 7" × 25½" (18 cm × 65 cm) rectangles. From the fusible interfacing, cut a 6" × 24¾" (15 cm × 63 cm) rectangle. From thin cotton batting, cut a 7" × 25½" (18 cm × 65 cm) rectangle.

2. Lay one muslin rectangle on a flat surface. Referring to the diagram, hand-baste seven lines, dividing the muslin into six pages, each 4" (10 cm) wide. Allow a ½" (1 cm) margin at the left edge and a 1" (3 cm) margin at the right edge.

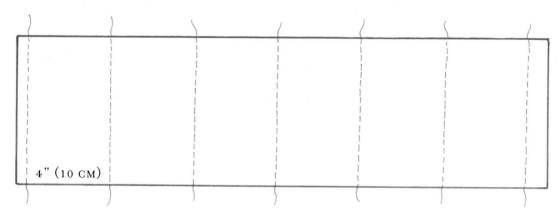

4" (10 CM)

Baste Guidelines

3. Arrange the image transfers on the marked muslin, one per page, in a sequence that you like. Trim each transfer to its final shape. The photos are trimmed close, with no white edge showing. The map and text are trimmed with a ⅜" (1 cm) margin all around. Hand-embroider or machine-stitch around the edges to hold each transfer in place. The sample project features ecru chain stitch around the map and group portrait, ecru feather-stitch around the oval portraits, and ecru lace edging around the annotation. Sew on bits of lace, ribbon insertion, buttons, and beads to decorate a blank page or to embellish the image transfer pages.

4. Place the iron-on interfacing on the wrong side of the second muslin rectangle, allowing for a 1" (3 cm) margin on one short end and a ½" (1 cm) margin around three sides. Fuse in place. Layer the two muslin pieces right sides together. Place the batting on top. Machine-stitch ½" (1 cm) from the edge around three sides, leaving the edge with the 1" (3 cm) margin open. Trim the batting as close to the stitching as possible. Also trim out the batting within the 1" (3 cm) margin to reduce bulk. Clip the corners. Turn right side out. Press. Machine-stitch along the basting lines through all layers to divide the piece into six pages. Remove the basting thread.

Assembling the Memory Book

Padded Foldout Pages

I. From the remaining cotton print, cut a 2" × 45" (5 cm × 114 cm) bias strip and a 1¼" × 20" (3.5 cm × 51 cm) bias strip; join shorter pieces if necessary to obtain the required length. From the cotton solid, cut an 8" × 11¾" (20 cm × 30 cm) rectangle. From the batting, cut two 8" × 11¾" (20 cm × 30 cm) rectangles. From the cardboard, cut a 6½" × 10¼" (17 cm × 25.5 cm) rectangle. Measure and mark two lines on the cardboard as shown. Score and fold on the marked lines.

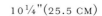
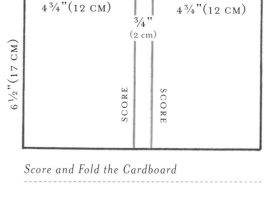

Score and Fold the Cardboard

2. Place the solid cotton rectangle right side up on a flat surface. Place the unfolded accordian pages facedown on top, 4¾" (12 cm) from the right edge and evenly spaced at the top and bottom, as shown. Stitch ½" (1 cm) from the raw edge through all layers. Trim the seam allowance to ¼" (0.5 cm). Fold the page piece over the seam allowance. Topstitch along the fold and again ⅜" (1 cm) from the fold through all layers.

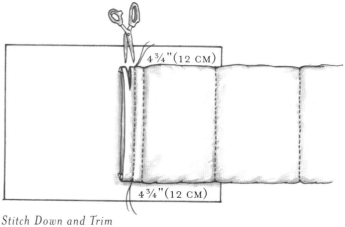

Stitch Down and Trim

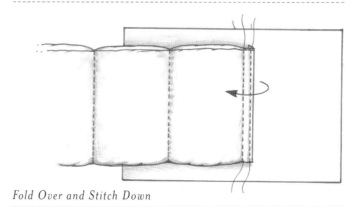

Fold Over and Stitch Down

3. Assemble the layers on a flat surface: crazy-quilt cover, facedown with crazy-patch at the left; batting; cardboard; batting; lining, faceup with accordian pages on the right. Pin through all layers, being sure to keep the cardboard centered. Machine-stitch ½" (1 cm) from the edge all around. Trim the seam allowance to ¼" (0.5 cm).

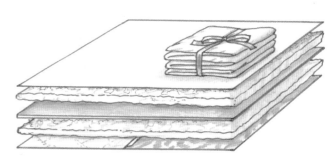

Layer the Pieces

4. Fold the wider bias strip lengthwise in half, wrong side in. Place the strip on the cover, raw edges matching. Stitch all around with a ¼" (0.5 cm) seam, leaving the ends loose. Stitch the loose ends together, trim off the excess, and complete the first seam. Turn the folded edge of the bias binding onto the lining and slipstitch in place, concealing the machine stitching.

5. Fold the remaining bias strip lengthwise in half, right side in. Machine-stitch the long edges together, making a ¼" (0.5 cm) seam. Press the seam allowance to one side. Trim the seam allowance slightly. Turn the strip right side out. Press with the seam centered. Cut into two 8½" (22 cm) strips and one 2" (5 cm) strip. Tuck in the ends of each strip, secure with fabric glue, and let dry. Glue the longer strips to the inside front and back covers for the book ties (see the project photograph). Fold and glue the shorter strip to the first accordion page as a pull-tab. Let the glue dry thoroughly before handling.

Denim Heart Tote

Betty Pillsbury

ARTIST

ABOUT THE PHOTO TRANSFERS

In 1990 while living in England, Betty Pillsbury came across a magazine article on crazy quilting. It proved to be a magic key, unlocking the door to an array of project ideas. Here, at last, she could focus her talents and interests into one enduring needleart. To create her unique and exquisite pieces, Betty searches through flea markets, antique stores, and online auctions. Images from vintage cigarette silks, postcards, Victorian calling cards, and similar gems are liberally sprinkled over her crazy quilt pieces.

Using a color digital copier and photo transfer paper, Betty photocopies the vintage ephemera and irons them onto cotton sateen or other appropriate fabrics for inclusion in her crazy quilt works. In this way, the original objects are preserved and can be used again and again. If you have no vintage pieces to copy, you might use wrapping paper, photographs, or copyright-free images from calendars, catalogs, and magazines.

MATERIALS

- denim tote bag, about 16" × 12" (41 cm × 30 cm)
- fancy silks, satins, jacquards
- 11" × 11" (28 cm × 28 cm) prewashed muslin (for foundation)
- 11" × 11" (28 cm × 28 cm) nonfusible interfacing
- vintage 5" (13 cm) round doily
- silk ribbon:
  $5/8$"-wide (1.5 cm) wired-edge hand-dyed green
  4mm antique olive
  4mm bright green
- 1 yard (0.9 m) dark gold metallic twisted cord
- assorted cotton, rayon, and metallic embroidery flosses
- tatted trim
- narrow ribbon flower trims
- bugle beads
- seed beads
- brass hummingbird charm
- monofilament sewing thread
- sewing thread

PHOTO TRANSFERS

- 3 vintage images
- white or cream cotton or silk fabric
- photo transfer supplies (see page 14)

TOOLS

- sewing machine
- steam iron
- sewing shears
- seam ripper
- computer with printer (optional)
- photocopier
- black fine-point permanent marker
- finely sharpened chalk pencil
- needles: sharps, embroidery, beading
- straight pins
- presscloth
- template-making supplies (see page 12)

INSTRUCTIONS

1. Review Photo Transfer Methods on page 14 and decide which method to follow. Use your images to make three photo transfers, each about 2" × 3" (5 cm × 8 cm), on white or cream cotton or silk fabric, or on printable fabric transfer sheets.

2. Photocopy the Large Heart pattern on page 23 at 185%, or so it measures about 9½" (24 cm) across. Use the enlarged pattern to make 1 Extra-Large Heart template.

3. Lay the muslin flat. Center the Extra-Large Heart template on the muslin and pin it in place. Trace the heart outline with a black fine-point permanent marker. Flip the muslin over. Retrace the heart outline on the back so it's visible from both sides.

4. Refer to Crazy-Patch on page 15. Stitch the fancy fabrics to the muslin, working from the center out. Use a presscloth and iron to press each seam from the right side as you go. Continue until the entire heart is covered. Make sure the final patches extend beyond the heart outline by at least ½" (1 cm).

5. Press the entire heart from the right side, using a presscloth to protect the fabrics. Carefully turn the work over. On the wrong side, machine-stitch just outside the heart outline all around, being careful not to distort the patches that extend beyond the outline. The stitching defines the heart shape and stabilizes the fabrics. Trim away the excess fabric ¼" (0.5 cm) beyond the stitching line.

6. Position one of the photo transfers from step 1 on the crazy-patch heart. Hand-appliqué in place. Hand-sew a ribbon flower trim around the edges to frame the picture.

7. Embellish every seam with embroidery stitches (see page 17), tatted trim, beads, or embroidered silk ribbon roses. Refer to the project photo for placement and color ideas. Develop your design according to your own fabrics and materials. Short lengths of lace can be tacked in place with needle and thread. Use a beading needle and thread to attach beads; for a string of beads, use a couching stitch.

8. Select empty areas of the crazy-quilt heart for further embellishment. Use a newly sharpened chalk pencil to draw a heart outline or write the word *Love*. Embroider over the marked lines in chain stitch. For a sparkly look, use rayon floss or 1 strand each of rayon and metallic floss. Tack on seed beads or small charms for added sparkle.

9. Use the Extra-Large Heart template to cut a heart from nonfusible interfacing. Use a seam ripper to cut a 3" (8 cm) vertical slit in the interfacing heart. Lay the crazy-quilt heart right side up on a flat surface. Lay the interfacing heart on top and pin around the edges. Machine-stitch ½" (1 cm) from the edge all around. Trim the seam allowance to ¼" (0.5 cm). Clip the curves. Turn right side out through the opening. Press.

Sew and Trim the Heart

10. Lay the denim tote flat. Arrange the crazy-quilt heart, vintage doily, and remaining photo transfers on the tote, overlapping them as shown in the project photograph. Pin through one layer of denim only. Use monofilament thread to hand-sew the pieces to the tote. Tack gold cord around the large heart. Embellish the edges of the photo transfers with blanket stitch or a ribbon rose trim.

Quilted Triptych

Lesley Riley

ARTIST

ABOUT THE PHOTO TRANSFERS

Lesley Riley began experimenting with image transfers long before today's inkjet and laser printing technologies were available. Her transparency method, described on page 15, creates transfers with a timeworn, aged look. For this triptych project, she uses contemporary supplies and materials.

To create a successful triptych design, decide on a theme and then search for images that relate well to the theme and to each other. The bird images used here, taken from vintage postcards, include songbird prints (complete with call notes!) and a young Victorian girl holding an empty birdcage. Paired with an apropos quotation, they express an ideal of freedom. A tiny brass bird winging its way overhead completes the sentiment.

If only I could so live and serve the world that
after me there should never again be birds in
cages. —Isak Dinesen

PHOTO TRANSFERS

- three vintage postcards or other copyright-free images
- quotation or words cut from magazine
- inkjet-printable fabric

MATERIALS

- ³/₈ yard (0.4 m) each of two different contrasting decorator fabrics (or two extra-large scraps)
- coordinating fabric scraps
- thin cotton batting
- acid-free matte board
- brass bird charm
- sewing thread
- craft glue

TOOLS

- computer with scanner and inkjet printer
- sewing machine
- steam iron
- sewing shears
- craft knife with sharp blade
- scissors
- metal straightedge
- ruler
- pencil
- sewing needle
- straight pins
- chalk pencil
- large sheet of paper (for template)

INSTRUCTIONS

I. Scan your vintage images and quotation. Resize the images, if necessary, to about 2½" × 4¼" (6 cm × 10.5 cm) each; resize the quotation to fit within a 1" × 3½" (3 cm × 9 cm) area. Use your computer's photo software to arrange several images on a page. Print the file on inkjet-printable fabric, following the manufacturer's instructions. Use sewing shears to cut out each piece ⅛" (0.3 cm) beyond the image area.

2. Use a ruler and pencil to mark one 6" × 10" (15 cm × 25 cm) and two 6" × 9" (15 cm × 23 cm) rectangles on matte board. Use a straightedge and a craft knife to cut out all three pieces. Mark two diagonal lines at one end of the larger rectangle as shown. Cut on the marked lines and discard the triangles to form a pediment.

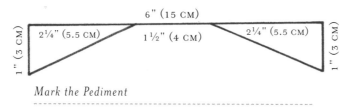

Mark the Pediment

3. To make a template, lay the three matte board panels side by side on a large sheet of paper. Allow about ¼" (0.5 cm) between the pieces. Use a pencil to trace around the entire triptych. Also draw lines in the spaces between the panels. Remove the panels and set them aside. Use a pencil and a ruler to true up the marked lines. Mark a new outline ⅜" (1 cm) beyond the first outline all around. Cut out the paper template on the outside line.

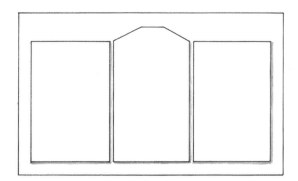

Make a Template

4. Layer two decorator fabrics and the thin cotton batting on a flat surface (in any order). Place the template on top and pin in place. Cut along the template edge through all the layers. Do not cut the pieces into separate panels.

5. Lay the batting flat. Lay the fabric for the front, or inside, of the triptych on top, right side up. Use a chalk pencil to lightly mark the lines for three panels, to match the template. Arrange a few fabric scraps and an image transfer on each panel. Overlap progressively smaller pieces for a framed effect. Keep the collage loose and playful by angling the pieces slightly. Pay attention to the overall balance and effect, but don't be overly fussy about straight edges or precise alignment. When you are satisfied with your arrangement, pin the pieces in place.

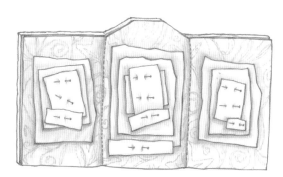

Create the Collage

6. Machine-stitch the collage pieces through all layers, using matching or contrasting thread. Leave the raw edges exposed. Fray some of the edges for a casual, timeworn look. Turn the work over. Trim off the excess batting just beyond the outermost stitching line of each panel.

7. Layer the front and back triptych fabrics right sides together and edges matching. Stitch the side and top edges with a ¼" (0.5 cm) seam; leave the bottom edge open. Clip the corners and points. Turn right side out. Press from the wrong side. Turn the bottom edge ⅜" (1 cm) to the inside and press. Machine-stitch along the chalk lines to create 3 pockets. Insert a matte board panel into each pocket. Sew the bottom closed by hand. Glue the bird charm to the middle panel.

Triptych Variation
Changing the size or shape of the panels lets you customize the triptych to fit any image. This version has a wider middle panel to accommodate a group photo.

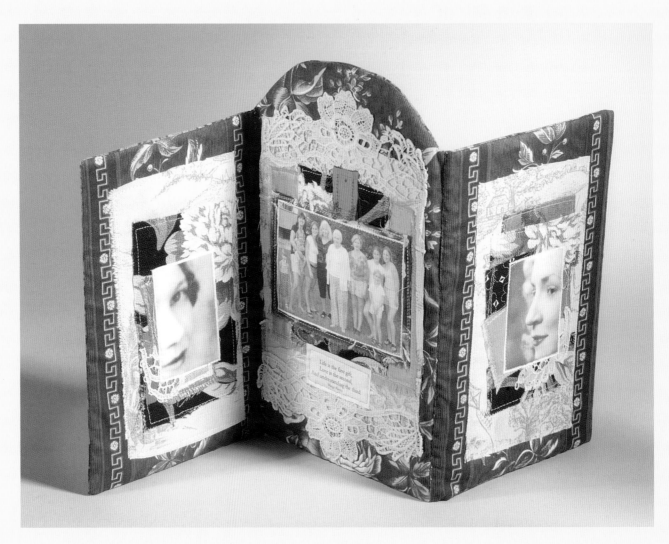

In step 2, cut the middle panel 6½" × 10½" (17 cm × 27 cm), or the desired size. Use a plate or bowl as a template to create the rounded top, as shown. Lace and netting overlays in the collage add to the feminine theme.

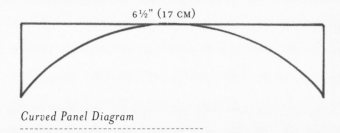

6½" (17 CM)

Curved Panel Diagram

Gallery

TWELVE MORE INSPIRING PROJECTS TO TEASE OUT
THE TREASURES IN YOUR STASH.

Leather Wall Hanging

Cindy Gorder
ARTIST

Soft sueded leathers form a backdrop for sparkly beads and threads in this crazy quilt extravaganza. The colorful leather patches overlap by ½" (1 cm) or more; the visible edges are cut with novelty scalloping shears. Some of the patches are stamped or printed with metallic inks.

Compared to fabric, leather is cumbersome to handle. Designer Cindy Gorder uses interfacing as a foundation and holds individual patches in place with tape or leather glue until the embroidery over the seams is complete. Rather than tape down the entire arrangement, she works on a few patches at a time, using a photograph of her initial design as a guide.

A sharp glover's needle and a rubber needle puller make the needling easier. A double strand of thread in a beading needle works fine for the beads. Hand-sewn leather medallions, shiny and frosted beads, a silver concho, and an iridescent peacock feather peeking out of a leather pocket complete this unusual collage.

Designed by Cindy Gorder for The Leather Factory/Tandy Leather

Crazy Quilt Vest

Linda Wyszynski

ARTIST

Crazy quilting doesn't have to go over the top to look beautiful. For this vest, designer Linda Wyszynski chose dressy black fabrics. Silk shantung, taffeta, moiré, and a woven floral pattern create an elegant tone-on-tone look. The shimmering blue-gray seam embellishment, embroidered with rayon and silk flosses, is just as subtle. Linda added sprays of flowers and a few daisy sprigs in some of the patches for a hint of color. The stitches used include lazy daisy, straight stitch, French knot, and bullion stitch.

To try this idea, choose a commercial vest pattern with flat, dart-free pieces. Use the pattern to cut muslin foundations for crazy quilting. As with all crazy quilting, start with a five-sided shape near the middle of the foundation and build out from there until the entire piece is covered. Finish the embellishment work before proceeding to the vest assembly.

Designed by Linda Wyszynski for Annie's Attic

Diploma Frame

Andrea Stern

ARTIST

Whether your degree is in basketweaving or nuclear physics, you'll enjoy making this fabric frame to display it. Folded fabric triangles work like old-fashioned photo album mounts to hold your sheepskin in place at the corners. The lightly padded textile sandwich is quilted with hand embroidery. Underneath the diploma, densely spiraled machine quilting helps the layers lie nice and flat. A pair of vintage floral embroideries, chain-stitched swirls, and a lacy edging mimic the fancy steel-engraved designs favored on diplomas just a generation or two ago.

Fabric artist Andrea Stern based this design on an earlier piece she made on commission. A fabric pocket on the back holds a piece of Plexiglas, allowing for display on a plate stand or tabletop easel. Another option is to sew a sleeve pocket on the back for a wall-mounted display.

Clipboard Cover

Beverly Fischer

ARTIST

Metallic threads burst out from the centers of gold and copper spirals in this dazzling fireworks display. Underneath lies the simple patchwork block that inspired it all. Done in pedestrian beiges and browns, the 9½" × 9½" (24 cm × 24 cm) block has 25 squares arranged in a 5-by-5 grid; it may have originally been made as a study in lights to darks. Designer Beverly Fischer bordered the block with a medium-tone print and then turned the whole thing slightly askew to create the fabric for her clipboard cover. This project is a perfect marriage between "out-there" design elements and utilitarian function. The raised metallic swirls and wild flyaway wisps make an ordinary office item fun to display and use. Other jazzy details include the gold-painted clip with its fan-shaped metallic spray. Clip a standard yellow pad directly over the embellishments and write away.

Happy Doll Pins

Barbara Evans

ARTIST

Patchwork odds and ends make perky gowns for this artsy doll jewelry by Barbara Evans. Each piece of patchwork is wrapped around a 5" (13 cm) strip of cardboard and sewn at the back. If a favorite scrap isn't big enough to reach all around, a piece of felt glued onto the back can hide the problem. A few judiciously placed hand stitches cinch and define the neck; a small beaded necklace would perform the same shaping magic.

Embellishments give a distinct personality to each doll. An unusual button or bead is a must for a prominent face. Experiment with seed beads and two-holed buttons to achieve whimsical eye contact. Beaded hairstyles include loopy seed bead strands, a flower and leaf headband, and long dangling tresses. A sequence of beads creates the illusion of shoulders, elbows, and hands, with muscles bulging out in all the appropriate places! To wear your creation, just attach a purchased pin back to the reverse side.

Quilted Vase

Lynne Sward

ARTIST

Part sculpture, part textile, Lynne Sward's stunning cylindrical vase depicts an underwater world teaming with fish and aquatic plants. Entitled *Under the Sea*, the vase truly does take you on a deep sea dive. A plunge through the scalloped waves on the surface takes you to the dark, mysterious waters of the deep.

The fish swim through layers of batiks, organzas, and cotton prints that are held together with machine and hand quilting and appliqué. Both straight and zigzag stitches wander freely across the surface. Sparkly metallic threads play up the shimmery organza and add to the interplay of light and shadow. More fish swim along the lining of the vase. You see them every time you fill the purchased glass liner that fits inside.

Cigar Box Art

Betty Auth

ARTIST

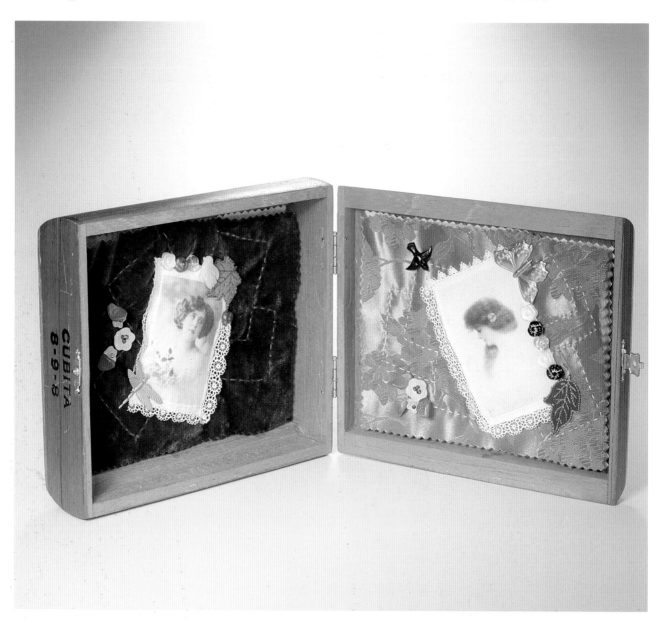

Betty Auth stood a cedar cigar box on its side to create this elegant diptych frame. Both the box interior and recessed lid are decorated with simple collages. Two image transfers, copied from early twentieth-century photographs and partially edged in lace, impart a vintage theme. Each transfer is sewn to a lightly padded, hand-quilted fabric background. Putting a darker velvet in the deeper recess and a lighter rose-toned fabric in the shallower lid recess plays up the shadowbox effect.

Both fabric collages are pinked around the edges and glued in place. Decorative buttons, brass charms, and small leaf appliqués add dimensional interest without overwhelming the space. When closed, this box could hold love letters, dried rose petals, or small items too precious to throw away.

Beaded Jewelry

Shannah Plutchak

ARTIST

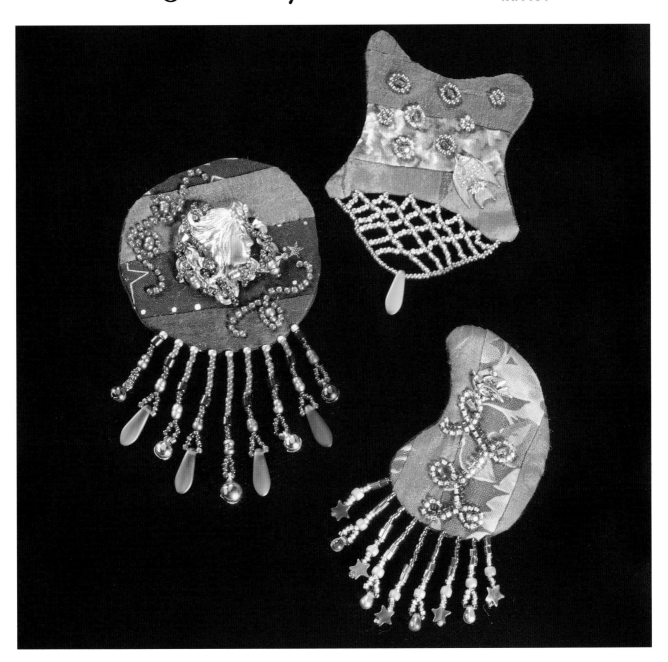

These quilt pin creations originated with Char Russell of Tabitha Quilts. Cottons and silks are strip-pieced to a flannel backing, cut into circles or quirky shapes, and lined with black cotton. Char's daughter, Shannah Plutchak, does the collage-style beading.

Shannah's bead selection runs the gamut. She expertly intermixes shiny with matte, smooth with faceted, clear with opaque. Some of the beads are couched to the fabric, while others dangle down in multiple strands or netted webs. Each pin also features a signature motif in the form of a brass charm. Favorites are wood nymphs, dragonflies, birds, and porpoises. The shape and adornments of these pins are reminiscent of military award medals or school blazer crests, but the aura is purely their own.

Created by Shannah Plutchak/Tabitha Quilts

Bell-Shaped Purse

Betty Pillsbury

ARTIST

Crystal beads, vintage buttons, and gorgeous ribbon and silk thread embroidery are just a sampling of the many adornments Betty Pillsbury has collaged in this delicate purse. The background fabrics, including vintage silks and satins, are chosen first and seamed together. Then Betty pores over her enormous stash to select just the right embellishments. She often runs a length of tatting or ribbon along the entire piece to tie the various fabric components together.

For those who love creating with needlework, small projects make perfect canvases. This old-fashioned design, reminiscent of a lady's reticule, or drawstring purse, uses four identical bell-shaped panels. Two of the panels are lavishly crazy-quilted, while the other two, cut from patterned silk, fold in at the sides. The interior is very roomy; a hidden closure at the top keeps the contents secure.

Freestanding Doll

Barbara Evans

ARTIST

A rectangle of Seminole-style patchwork, left over from a project by Jessica Prescott, inspired this doll design by Barbara Evans. The supporting frame couldn't be simpler: a dowel for the body, a bamboo skewer for the arms, and a wooden plaque for the base. The head is fashioned by joining two fabric-covered cardboard ovals back-to-back.

The creative genius comes with the embellishing, and this doll was made for display. Glass butterfly and flower beads, vintage buttons, and drop earrings are some of the treasures on view. The outstretched arms offer ready-made gallery space for all sorts of doodads. Black tassel hair and milagros hands make a humorous play at realism. A tiny brass mask keeps this Mardi Gras girl's identity under wraps, but she has plenty of other charms to amuse you.

Patchwork by Jessica Prescott

Quilted Box with Lid

Lynne Sward

ARTIST

Another of Lynne Sward's signature fabric sculptures, this soft trapezoidal box is self-supporting because of the inward-sloping walls. The box walls and base are sewn from hand-dyed fabrics layered with flannel and craft foam for added stiffness. Small "postage stamp" photo transfers are machine-zigzagged across the surface. The effect is of a miniature picture gallery.

The lid in this mixed media piece is papier-mâché over a cardboard armature. A reverse lip on the lid interior fits into the box opening. Turquoise paint and color photocopies of the pictures match the box so closely, it's hard to tell the two pieces were constructed differently. The complete work has a touch-me quality. Is the lid soft, or is the box rigid?

Three Wall Pieces

Andrea Stern

ARTIST

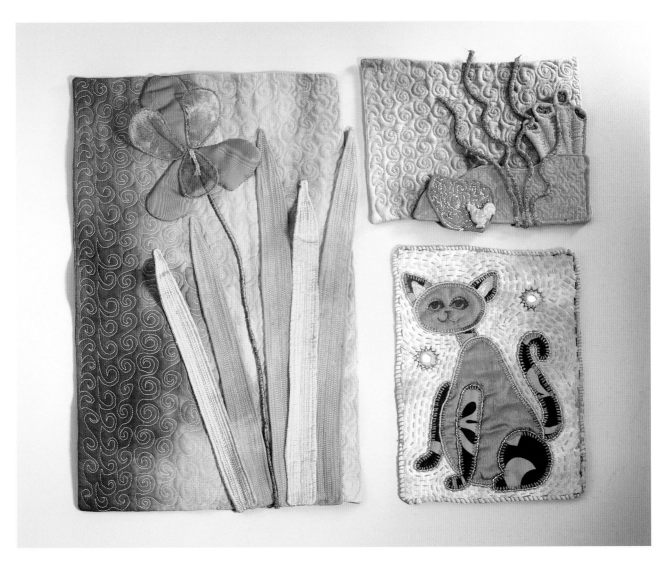

Andrea Stern's three small works of art—the largest is 10" × 16" (25 cm × 41 cm)—all use densely packed quilting and complementary colors to heighten the visual intensity.

In *Spring Glory*, column upon column of continuous spiral and wave patterns advance across a hand-dyed background. This violet-to-yellow cloth was acquired by the designer through a fabric-of-the-month club. The purple iris is sewn from moiré and silk organza. Up to 12 lines of yellow-green stitching pack each spear-shaped leaf.

Chicken of the Sea is a red-and-green experimental piece. Corals and underwater formations are sewn from red silks and cot-tons and then applied, collage-style, to the watery machine-quilted background. Machine-made cording functions as slender coral branches. The tiny turquoise chicken sat languishing in Andrea's stash for years waiting for this project to come along.

In *Rockabye Kitty*, blue meets orange. The bold cat shapes are cut from silk dupioni and a cotton print; variegated floss and couched seed beads electrify the edges. In the background, big pearl cotton hand stitching echoes the cat contours as it quilts the layers together. You can practically feel this hand-dyed silk dupioni vibrate with energy.

Artist Directory

Annette Calhoun
1890 26th Avenue NW
New Brighton, MN 55112 USA
*Annette Calhoun is a seamstress and fin-
isher who often collaborates with designer
Linda Wyszynski to create new projects.*

Pat Claus
120 Churchdale Ave. N.
Keizer, OR 97303 USA
503-393-1111
*Pat Claus is an avid quilter. She loves to
work on projects that combine painting and
quilting.*

Barbara Evans
124 Poli Street
Ventura, CA 93001 USA
805-648-3860
805-643-5517 (fax)
BarbEDolls@aol.com
*Barbara Evans is a doll artist and teacher.
She designs in cloth and handmade felt and
loves the challenge of incorporating found
materials in her creations. Currently,
paper dolls have taken center stage, and
Barbara's students are learning how to
design paper dolls with hidden articulated
joints. Barbara's work is featured in books,
magazines, and numerous venues, including
galleries, stores, and cloth doll conferences.*

Beverly Fischer
Bev at Home Designs
619 N.E. 1st Avenue
Galva, IL 61434 USA
309-932-9971
beverly@theinter.com
*Beverly Fischer is trained in interior design
and has extensive experience working with
fabrics. Over the years, she has created
various items in the gift field, including
clothing, soft home furnishings, and wall
hangings. A new venture is the acquisition
of a 110-year-old home in central
Illinois. Beverly is redecorating the house
in a simplified style to reflect the early
Swedish settlement of the area. She plans to
eventually open it as a bed-and-breakfast.*

Valerie Fontenot
3500 East Simcoe, #22
Lafayette, LA 70501 USA
337-237-2065
*Valerie Fontenot has collaborated with her
mother, Betty Auth, on various design
projects over the years.*

Cindy Gorder
Mineral Point, WI 53565 USA
*Cindy Gorder is both a professional
graphic artist and a craft designer. She has
always been interested in collage and crazy
quilting. Crazy quilting opened the door to
beadwork. Cindy enjoys a rural lifestyle
with her husband on his Wisconsin dairy
farm.*

Judi Kauffman
judineedle@aol.com
*Judi Kauffman is a versatile designer,
author, and teacher who freelances for
almost twenty magazines as well as several
manufacturers. Her specialties include
needlepoint, embroidery, piecework,
rubber stamping, paper arts, and collage.
She teaches drawing at The Corcoran
College of Art & Design.*

Gretchen Nutt
Florilegium Antiques and
Needleart
823 East Johnson Street
Madison, WI 53703 USA
608-256-7310
floril@florilegium.com
www.florilegium.com
*Gretchen Nutt is a recovering accountant
who can never be found without a needle
in her hand. Her store specializes in
antique needlework, crazy quilts, beadwork, trims, and ribbons. Her crazy quilt
square was featured on the cover of the
2002 Quilting Arts Calendar.*

Carla J. Peery
Carla J. Peery Design
20133 42nd Avenue NE
Lake Forest Park, WA 98155 USA
206-365-8912
206-595-9717 (cell)
cpeerysew@aol.com
*Carla J. Peery has been experimenting with
fabrics since she was a small child. A sewing
teacher, lecturer, and fabric artist, she
specializes in beginning sewing and quilting
instruction for both children and adults.
Carla teaches through a variety of pro-
grams in the greater Seattle area, and she
also travels and teaches silk dyeing and
painting at sewing seminars around the
United States.*

Betty Pillsbury
166 Coon's Road
Middleburgh, NY 12122 USA
518-827-8730
bpills@midtel.net
www.bettypillsbury.com

Betty Pillsbury is an award-winning needle artist and teacher who taught herself how to embroider when she was eight years old. Her passion for needlework led her to explore all sorts of embroidery techniques, including the crazy quilting that has become her specialty. Betty has appeared on HGTV's Simply Quilts and the PBS show Quilt Nebraska, and her work has been featured in galleries and publications nationwide. She is currently renovating a barn at her home in New York State, where she plans to hold classes.

Shannah Plutchak

Tabitha Quilts
978-264-0611
www.Tabithaquilts.com
Shannah Plutchak is the author of the step-by-step instructions included in every beginner Tiny Quilt Pin kit. (The kits are available for purchase from Tabitha Quilts; see page 111.)

Lesley Riley

7814 Hampden Lane
Bethesda, MD 20814 USA
LRileyART@aol.com
www.LaLasLand.com
Best known for her Fragment series of small fabric collages, Lesley is a nationally known quilter, dollmaker, and mixed media artist with a dual passion for color and the written word. Lesley's transfer methods and creative work have been featured in today's premiere quilting, art, stamping, and doll magazines. Lesley hopes that her art and website (www.LaLasLand.com) will inspire others to find their own voice and to create from the heart.

Dee Stark

705 Brandywine Parkway
Guilderland, NY 12084 USA
518-869-5740
dee@deestark.com
www.deestark.com
Dee Stark is a textile artist with a special interest in techniques popular from 1860 to 1920, including crazy quilting, lace-making, and silk ribbon embroidery. She is author of A Spiderweb for Luck: Symbols & Motifs used in Crazy Quilting, a regular feature editor of the Crazy Quilt Society Newsletter, and a contributor to the online Crazy Quilt Magazine. More recently, she has undertaken traditional appliqué quilting and art and landscape quilts. Dee is avidly sought as lecturer and instructor at quilt and textile shows in the United States and abroad.

Andrea Stern

P.O. Box 559
Chauncey, OH 45719 USA
740-797-3016
polymer@frognet.net
www.embellishmentcafe.com
Andrea Stern designs in a range of media, from bead embroidery to art quilts. Her work has won numerous awards and appeared in many publications. She has owned her own bead business since 1991.

Lynne Sward

625 Bishop Drive
Virginia Beach, VA 23455 USA
757-497-7917
lssward@erols.com
Lynne Sward uses cloth, threads, beads, paper, and other media to create one-of-a-kind art works that reflect her interest in ethnic cultures. Her pieces can be seen in national and international shows and galleries on the East Coast. Lynne loves sharing her enthusiasm and unique talents with others. Her work has been featured in over twelve books, including Making Creative Cloth Dolls by Marthe LeVann, and in Quilting Arts Magazine. Her studios at home and in Norfolk, Virginia, are Lynne's special sanctuaries where she connects daily with her muses.

Linda Wyszynski

7200 Glenwood Avenue
Golden Valley, MN 55427 USA
763-545-1009
Linda@HearthsideCreations.net
Linda Wyszynski is a nationally recognized needlework designer and teacher. Her cross-stitch, silk ribbon, needlepoint, embroidery, and stamping designs have appeared in more than a dozen books and numerous magazines, including Bridal 101, Better Homes and Gardens, NeedleArts, and Romantic Living. Linda has served on the board of directors for the Society of Craft Designers, the Minnesota Chapter of Embroiderers' Guild of America, the Minneapolis/St. Paul Metropolitan Art Council, and the Polk County Art Council. She currently teaches two Needlepoint Group Correspondence Courses for the EGA.

Product Resource Guide

This guide is organized by both project and vendor. Look under the project name to find out more about the particular materials and products used. For further information, or to purchase a product, consult the vendor listing that follows. Materials and products not listed below are either readily available or came from the designer's stash.

PROJECTS

page 20
Embroidered Needlebooks
Unique hand-dyed fabrics and conversation prints from Lunn Fabrics. Bugle beads from The Embellishment Café. Batting from Quilters Dream Poly. Turn-It-All tool from Elinor Peace Bailey.

page 28
Quilt Block Heart Pillow
Nymo D beading thread from Pepperell Pepper Patch Works. Fiberfill from Fairfield. Beacon Fabri-Tac adhesive from Joann. Stop Fraying from Aleene's.

page 34
Collage Jewelry Box
Wooden musical jewelry box #99451 from Sudberry House. Glass dragonfly #12285 and Magnifica beads #10017 from Mill Hill Beads. Shimmer Sheetz iridescent Mylar sheets from Sulyn Industries. Beacon Gem-Tac and Fabri-Tac adhesives from Joann. Blopens fabric pens from P & M Color Workshop. Butterfly punch from McGill Craftivity. Fiskars Soft-Grip flower punch from Joann.

page 40
A Box of Jewels
Nymo D beading thread from Pepperell Pepper Patch Works. Schmetz metallica #80/12 needle from Nancy's Notions.

page 46
Footstool Slipcover
Pebeo Cobalt Blue, Fuchsia, Buttercup, Vermillion, Ultramarine Blue, Emerald Green, Violet, and Turquoise fabric paints, Deka opaque white paint from Dharma Trading Company. Loew-Cornell pointed round liner brush #795 from Pearl Paint.

page 58
Velvet Pincushions
Rayon/silk velvet (white and hand-dyed), silk ribbon (white and hand-dyed), Czech pressed glass beads, and silk buttonhole twist from Florilegium Antiques & Needleart. Pebeo Soie dyes available from Dharma Trading Company and PRO Chemical & Dye Co.

page 66
Silk Brocade Purse
Gold purse frame and chain from Lacis. Colorhue dyes, Tire 100# silk thread, and Tire quilter's silk from Things Japanese. Beads from Beadcats.

page 72
Silk and Satin Bottle Covers
Assorted fabrics from Cindy Brick, eQuilter, The Kirk Collection, and Pepperell Pepper Patch Works. Vintage buttons and beads from Tinsel Trading Company and TWE Beads. Silk threads, floss, and ribbon from Victoria Clayton, Dyer.

page 78
Accordian-Fold Memory Book
Avery-Dennison inkjet cotton printable fabric from The Fabric Club. Pellon fusible interfacing #911FF. Soft Touch cotton batting from Fairfield Processing. Very fine #4 braid, gold #002, from Kreinik Mfg. Co. Inc. Ecru floss from DMC. Sew Perfect Lace 1" (3 cm) rayon seam binding #5993 and ¼" (0.5 cm) cotton lace #HL 3049-96 from Hancock Fabrics. La-petite #99 ½" mother-of-pearl buttons and La Mode ½" (1 cm) shell-style buttons #46690 from Blumenthal-Lansing Company. Small bugle beads and glass seed beads from Mill Hill Beads. Beacon Fabri-Tac permanent adhesive from Joann.

page 86
Denim Tote
Photo transfers from Betty Pillsbury. Denim tote and gold metallic twisted cord from Joann. Fabrics from eQuilter. Silk ribbons from Victoria Clayton, Dyer, and Vintage Vogue. Threads from Pepperell Pepper Patch Works. Trims from Maureen Greeson.

page 96
Leather Wall Hanging
Leather and suede patches, lacing, leather strips, beaded rosettes, spots, conchos, leather shears, glover's needles, leather cement from The Leather Factory. Metallic braid and FacetsT beadlike yarn from Kreinik.

page 99
Clipboard Cover
Big Swirl #D051 stamp from Hot Potatoes. Enhancers Textile Medium from Aleene's. Quick Stitch Foil Glue and Metallic Fabric Foil from Jones Tones Inc. Gold metallic and copper metallic floss from DMC. Antique gold fabric paint from Pearl Paint. Folk Art paint #660 Metallic Pure Gold from Plaid Enterprises, Inc.

page 100
Happy Doll Pins
Flower and leaf beads from Beadcats.

page 103
Beaded Jewelry
Kits for making pins available from Tabitha Quilts.

page 104
Bell-Shaped Purse
Fabrics from eQuilter. Cording from Joann. Trims and buttons from Maureen Greeson. Threads from Pepperell Pepper Patch Works. Ribbons from Victoria Clayton, Dyer, and Vintage Vogue.

page 105
Freestanding Doll
Flower and leaf beads from Beadcats. Black iridescent seed beads from BeadTime.

VENDORS

Aleene's
800-438-6226
aleenes.com

Ballarat Patchwork
54 Victoria Street
Ballarat, 3350
Victoria, Australia
61 3 5332 6722
www.ballaratpatchwork.com.au

Barossa Quilt & Craft Cottage
Box 458
Angaston
South Australia 5353
61 8 8562 3212
www.barossaquilt.com.au

Beadcats
The Universal
Synergetics, Inc. Bead
Store
503-625-2323
www.beadcats.com

BeadTime
4572 Telephone Road
#915
Ventura, CA 93003
USA
805-658-6323
www.beadtime.com

Betty Pillsbury
www.bettypillsbury.com

Blumenthal-Lansing Company
1929 Main Street
Lansing, IA 52151
USA
563-538-4211
www.buttonsplus.com

Cindy Brick
www.cindybrick.com

Dharma Trading Company
800-542-5227
www.dharmatrading.com

The DMC Corporation
Port Kearney Bldg. 10
South Kearney, NJ 07032
USA
973-589-0606
www.dmc-usa.com

Elinor Peace Bailey
1779 East Avenue
Hayward, CA 94541
USA
510-582-2702
www.epbdolls.com

The Embellishment Café
P.O. Box 186
The Plains, OH 45780
USA
740-797-3153
www.embellishmentcafe.com

eQuilter
877-FABRIC-3 or
303-527-0856
www.equilter.com

The Fabric Club
P.O. Box 767670
Roswell, GA 30078
USA
800-322-2582
www.fabricclub.com

Fairfield Processing
P. O. Box 1157
Danbury, CT 06813
USA
800-980-8000
www.poly-fil.com

Florilegium Antiques & Needleart
823 East Johnson Street
Madison, WI 53703
USA
608-256-7310
www.florilegium.com

Hancock Fabrics
www.hancockfabrics.com

Hot Potatoes
www.hotpotatoes.com

Joann
www.joann.com

Jones Tones
www.jonestones.com

The Kirk Collection
www.kirkcollection.com

Kreinik Mfg. Co. Inc.
800-537-2166
www.kreinik.com

Lacis
33163 AdelineStreet
Berkeley, CA 94703
USA
510-843-7178
www.lacis.com

The Leather Factory/Tandy Leather Company
P.O. Box 50429
Fort Worth, TX 76105
USA
800-433-3201
www.leatherfactory.com

Lunn Fabrics
317 E. Main Street
Lancaster, OH 43130
USA
800-880-1738
www.lunnfabrics.com

Maureen Greeson
www.maureengreeson.com

McGill Craftivity
www.mcgillinc.com
800-982-9884

Mill Hill Beads
P.O. Box 1060
Janesville, WI 53547
USA
800-356-9438
www.millhillbeads.com

Nancy's Notions
1-800-833-0690
www.nancysnotions.com

P & M Color Workshop
888-661-9421
www.blopens.com

Patchwork Gallery
17 Mead Close
Knutsford, Chesire
WA16 0OU
United Kingdom
01565 632553
www.patchworkgallery.co.uk

Pearl Paint Company
308 Canal Street
New York, NY 10013
USA
800-451-PEARL
www.pearlpaint.com

Pellon
pellonideas.com

Pepperell Pepper Patch Works
152 Main Street
Pepperell, MA 01463
USA
888-597-7771
www.pppatch.com

Plaid Enterprises, Inc.
800-842-4197
plaidonline.com

PRO Chemical & Dye Co.
800-228-9393
www.prochemical.com

Quilters Dream Poly
888-268-8664
quiltersdreambatting.com

Sudberry House
860-739-6951
www.sudberry.com

Sulyn Industries
800-25-SULYN

Tabitha Quilts
978-264-0611
www.Tabithaquilts

Things Japanese
425-821-2287
www.silkthings.com

Tinsel Trading Company
47 West 38th Street
New York, NY 10018
USA
212-730-1030
www.tinseltrading.com

TWE Beads
P.O. Box 55
Hamburg, NJ 07419
USA
www.twebeads.com

Victoria Clayton, Dyer
6448 Freeman Road
Bryon, NY 14422
USA
585-548-2620
www.hand-dyedfibers.com

Vintage Vogue
www.vintagevogue.com

About the Authors

Betty Auth, a passionate collector of quilt scraps and stash, has designed more than 300 projects for contributor books, national magazines, and online websites. She is the author of over 10 craft books, including *Stamping Tricks for Scrapbooks* (Rockport 2002). Betty participated in the craft industry as a columnist, feature writer, and guest on home and garden television shows. She held leadership roles in the Society of Craft Designers and coordinated Designs For Living, a major designer display at the annual ACCI Trade Show in Chicago.

Candie Frankel is the author of 8 how-to craft and decorating books, including *Babies' and Children's Rooms* and the *Encyclopedia of Country Furniture*. Her editorial credits include *McCall's Needlework & Crafts* and *Handcraft Illustrated* magazines, as well as books by today's top quilters, crafters, and needle artists.

Acknowledgments

Special thanks to Patricia Chatham Bolton, editor-in-chief of *Quilting Arts Magazine*, who worked with Betty Auth to invite several of the contributing artists to participate in this project.